PROGRAM DEBUGGING ENVIRONMENTS
Design and Utilization

ELLIS HORWOOD SERIES IN INTERACTIVE INFORMATION SYSTEMS

General Editor: V. A. J. MALLER, ICL Professor of Computer Systems, Loughborough University of Technology; formerly Technical Director, Thorn EMI Information Technology Ltd
Consulting Editors: Dr JOHN M. M. PINKERTON, Information Technology Consultant, J & H Pinkerton Associates, and formerly Manager of Strategic Requirements, International Computers Limited; and PATRICK HOLLIGAN, Department of Computer Science, Loughborough University of Technology

PROGRAM DEBUGGING ENVIRONMENTS
Design and Utilization

BEATRICE LAZZERINI
Dipartimento di Ingegneria della Informazione:
Elettronica, Informatica, Telecomunicazioni,
Università di Pisa, Italy
LANFRANCO LOPRIORE
Dipartimento di Ingegneria della Informazione:
Elettronica, Informatica, Telecomunicazioni,
Università di Pisa, Italy

ELLIS HORWOOD
NEW YORK   LONDON   TORONTO   SYDNEY   TOKYO   SINGAPORE

First published in 1992 by
ELLIS HORWOOD LIMITED
Market Cross House, Cooper Street,
Chichester, West Sussex, PO19 1EB, England

A division of
Simon & Schuster International Group
A Paramount Communications Company

Printed and bound in Great Britain
by Bookcraft, Midsomer Norton

British Library Cataloguing in Publication Data

A catalogue record for this book is available from the the British Library

ISBN 0–13–721838–9

Library of Congress Cataloging-in-Publication Data

Available from the publishers

Ada is a registered trademark of the U.S. Government, Ada Joint Program Office.

Contents

List of figures

Preface

A high level of complexity is involved in program dynamics. This is especially true for concurrent programs of even moderate size. A consequence of this complexity is the high cost in time of the debugging phase of program development. This book focuses on the activities involved in this phase, i.e. the diagnosis, localization and removal of program errors.

The book contains an extensive analysis of the techniques that have been devised to monitor the various aspects of program behaviour. We give a considerable emphasis to problem solving through the presentation of a large number of program debugging problems with their possible solutions. We focus on programs written in block-structured high-level languages. Special attention is paid to concurrent programs on account of the widespread popularity of concurrent programming languages over the last few years. Both shared-variable and message-passing concurrent languages are considered.

The analysis concentrates on the tools which can be used in the various stages of the program debugging process. The advantages resulting from the integration of these tools in a program debugging environment are evidenced, especially from the point of view of an effective implementation of the various debugging techniques. The environment design is considered in depth. An environment is presented which is largely independent of both the programming language and the operating system, and can be used to develop sequential and concurrent programs written in block-oriented languages.

READERSHIP

The book is aimed at programmers, and at researchers involved in the design of a program debugging environment. In particular, the programmer should obtain a deeper knowledge of the techniques used most widely in the debugging of both sequential and concurrent programs. These techniques are illustrated with reference to significant sample programs, through a large number of practical applications presented in the form of program debugging problems. The book is also intended for those users who are not computer professionals but who write their own programs.

The designer of a program debugging environment should find the analysis of a wide, congruent set of functionalities and services useful as it can represent a suitable base for the environment definition. The sample problems should assist him in assessing each functionality with respect to practical applications. He will be facilitated in the task of deciding whether a given functionality should be included in his implementation of the environment or not, by taking the specific requisites into account, and evaluating the benefits deriving from inclusion, and the loss of expressive power deriving from omission, of that functionality.

The book should also help the member of a software development group involved in, or influencing, the specification, selection or purchase authorization of software tools for high-level language program development. In this book, he will find a detailed analysis of the requisites for a program debugging environment in view of an effective support to the solution of real program debugging problems. Furthermore, the book can be useful reading for the manager who feels the need for a deep, up-to-date knowledge of advanced topics in programming and program development methodologies.

As far as the classroom is concerned, the book could be employed as a subsidiary textbook in undergraduate courses or the preliminary stages of postgraduate courses on programming techniques, programming languages and software engineering. It should also be suitable for postdegree courses for graduates converting from other disciplines.

The book assumes a grounding in computer programming, such as that which is typically obtained in a traditional first-year undergraduate course in Computer Science. Pascal is used as the example language. When a programming language concept not featured by Pascal is examined, a self-explanatory language derived from Pascal is used. In particular, this is the case for concurrent programs, which are considered in particular depth throughout the book.

ORGANIZATION

The book is divided into two main parts. Part I has been written by Lanfranco Lopriore and Part II by Beatrice Lazzerini.

Part I analyses a number of important aspects of the user interface of an effective program debugging environment, and outlines the services which the environment should provide. The issues considered include the environment architecture (Chapter 1), the identification of the program entities (Chapter 2), the monitoring of the program activity (Chapter 3), the management and utilization of the private storage of the environment (Chapter 4), and the definition of the layout of the program debugging experiment (Chapter 5). Each chapter includes several examples, aimed at clarifying the expressive power and the possible utilizations of the functionalities of the environment.

Part II demonstrates that a program debugging environment satisfying the requisites identified in Part I offers the user a considerable degree of control over the experiments, can be profitably used in the implementation of different monitoring techniques, and is effective in the analysis of complex aspects of program behaviour. Chapter 6 considers the debugging of sequential programs, while Chapters 7 and 8 consider the debugging of shared-variable and message-passing concurrent programs. Finally, Chapter 9 deals with program performance evaluation and the treatment of performance bugs. These chapters discuss several problems, reflecting a wide range of the type of situations which are likely to occur in the program debugging process. For each problem, a solution is given which aims at illustrating the utilization of the programming environment in a practical experiment of software debugging.

Part I

The design of a program debugging environment

Contents

Chapter 1

Introduction

Objective

This chapter summarizes the activities involved in the program debugging process, and introduces the tools used in this process to monitor the various aspects of program behaviour. The motivations for integrating these tools in a program debugging environment are briefly discussed, and the structure and the functionalities of the environment are presented.

Contents

1.1   THE PROGRAM DEBUGGING PROCESS

Debugging is the process of diagnosing, locating and removing program errors. After a program has been written, it is executed using carefully selected test data [Parrington, 1989]. If the program does not behave as expected, an error is suspected. The results of the execution are analysed, and the possible causes of the problem are hypothesized. A correction is proposed, and the tests are repeated. This process is iterated until a valid solution is found [McDowell, 1989], [Mullerburg, 1983]. Thus, the debugging process is a sequence of *debugging experiments*, each consisting of a set of tests aimed at obtaining answers to questions concerning the program behaviour.

1.1.1 The program state

The debugging process has a high time cost [Myers, 1976]. This is essentially a consequence of the high complexity of program dynamics [Binder, 1985]. In the *state-based* approach, the dynamics of the program under development (the *target program*) is observed from the point of view of the *program state*, i.e. the values of the program-defined entities, and the point reached by the program *control flow*. This is the sequence of statements which are executed as a consequence of the program activity. The *state history* is the evolution of an aspect of the program state expressed in terms of the values assumed by a subset of the program-defined entities. The *flow history* is the evolution of an aspect of the program state expressed in terms of the path followed by the program control flow.

If we repeatedly execute a given sequential program with the same given set of input data, we always obtain the same state and flow histories. This reproducible behaviour [Kaner, 1988] cannot be guaranteed for concurrent programs [Griffin, 1988], neither in a multiprocessor environment where the processes execute on different processors at different speeds, nor even in a single-processor environment, where the processor is switched among the processes, as a consequence of scheduling delays, of the non-deterministic nature of process interactions, and of the lack of synchronization between the activities of the processes.

1.1.2 Debugging techniques and tools

The state of the target program can be monitored by deviating the normal program control flow [Gondzio, 1987]. This effect will be obtained by inserting *traps*. A *break trap* is a permanent deviation which can be caused by the programmer from the console (*asynchronous* break trap), or by an aspect of the program activity (*synchronous* break trap). On a trap of this type, the program execution is suspended. The programmer can then inspect the program state by displaying the value of the program entities at the console, and also change the normal program execution if he wishes by altering the value of these entities.

A *trace trap* is a temporary deviation in the program control flow which causes the information concerning an aspect of the program state to be collected. This information can be displayed at the console, or, alternatively, can be recorded on a storage device for later analysis. A *trace* is the result of the information gathering actions generated by a sequence of trace traps. A *state trace* contains information concerning the program state history, and a *flow trace* contains information concerning the program flow history.

Break traps allow an effective control over the layout of the debugging experiment. At a trap of this type, the programmer can dynamically decide the items to be displayed. He can also insert new traps or eliminate existing traps. On the other hand, in the debugging of concurrent programs, break traps may be scarcely effective, and traces are likely to play a preeminent role [Gait, 1985], [Garcia-Molina, 1984]. Essentially, this is a consequence of the lack of reproducible behaviour, as the symptoms of an error in a concurrent program may not appear when the program is reexecuted [McDowell, 1989].

In the simplest form, the programmer can insert traps manually, by adding *debugging probes*, i.e. statements aimed at capturing debugging information, at appropriate points in the source code of the target program [Cheung, 1990], [Moher, 1988]. For instance, a trace trap can be implemented by inserting an output statement or a call to a trace-collecting subroutine which will produce a snapshot of selected components of the program state. This slow technique requires considerable manual intervention by the programmer [Einbu, 1989]. The output statements themselves are prone to errors, and this complicates the debugging activity.

The need to facilitate trap insertion is a first, important reason for the introduction of *ad-hoc* debugging tools. These tools support the different debugging techniques which have been devised to guide the programmer in mastering the complexity of program dynamics [Johnson, 1982], [Lauesen, 1979], [Myers, 1979]. A first example is an *execution monitor* aimed at supporting trace gathering. The list of the aspects of the target program activity to be actually traced can be part of the design of the monitor. This *automatic tracing* has a high cost in terms of the time required to gather the trace and the space required to store it, especially for concurrent programs for which we have to trace the activity of several processes [Garcia-Molina, 1984]. More sophisticated monitors feature filtering capabilities, which allow the programmer to select the aspects of the program activity which are of specific interest to the tracing experiment being performed (*selective tracing*). For instance, a state trace can be collected in terms of the values assumed by a small subset of the program entities, and a flow trace can be collected at a low level of granularity, e.g. branches, or subroutine invocations.

An *interactive debugging tool* makes it possible to interact with the target program during execution by means of break traps [Myers, 1976]. Usually, the programmer specifies the condition on the program state which causes generation of a break trap in terms of the execution of a given program statement. In this case, the trap is called a *breakpoint*. Most interactive debugging tools also make it possible to specify *single-step execution*, i.e. generation of a break trap on the execution of every program statement, or, possibly, of every statement of a given program fragment. This is useful especially when it is not clear where to place breakpoints [Elliot, 1982].

Many programs have performance objectives. An *execution profiler* is a tool specifically directed towards the detection and elimination of the causes of the limitations in program performance (*performance bugs*) [Ferrari, 1978], [McKerrow, 1988]. The profiler observes the program activity and evaluates the number of times a given statement or block is executed, for instance, or the number of calls to each subroutine or program module [Foxley, 1978], [Ponder, 1988]. This information will be used to determine the portions of the program source code which are responsible for high execution time costs.

1.1.3   Program debugging environments

If the programmer's activity is to be supported by a fixed collection of tools, each designed to implement a specific debugging technique, the effectiveness of these tools to cover all user needs is certainly a critical design aspect. Another problem is language independence. A multi-lingual debugging tool would allow the programmer involved in the development of a multi-lingual application, for instance an application integrating packages written in different languages, to learn only one debugging command set [Seidner, 1983]. However, few debugging tools support more than one high level language. This is especially true for the tools for the debugging of concurrent programs, which are often strongly oriented towards a specific construct for process interactions [Andrews, 1983], [Silberschatz, 1991].

In a different approach, the target program is executed under the control of a *debugging environment* featuring a powerful set of low-level primitives which can be compounded to form specialized tools [Lopriore, 1989], [van der Linden, 1985]. A possible interface between the environment and the target program uses *events* and *actions* [Bhatt, 1982], [Lazzerini, 1989b]. An event is the specification of a condition concerning an aspect of the program state and activity. On the occurrence of a given event, the debugging environment will perform the actions connected with that event. The command set of the debugging environment will include the commands to define events and actions, and to control the connections between the events and the actions.

Actions can involve the state of the debugging environment; examples are the storage of partial results into the private storage of the environment, or the modification of the layout of the debugging experiment dynamically. Actions can also involve the state of the target program, for instance, the generation of a trace trap aimed at displaying the values of a number of program-defined entities, or even the modification of these values, thereby altering the program state.

This book discusses the design and utilization of a program debugging environment (*PDE* from now on) in this second approach. PDE allows the programmer to monitor the program behaviour by expressing abstract specifications of selected aspects of the program dynamics, using a set of low-level, concrete mechanisms to inspect these dynamics. In this way, PDE can be employed to implement all widely used debugging techniques, and to evaluate all the usual program performance indexes. It is independent of the programming language, supporting both sequential and concurrent block-oriented high level languages.

1.2   PDE OVERVIEW

Figure 1.1 shows the PDE architecture and evidences the interactions of PDE with the target program. The target program is executed in a controlled fashion, according to the layout of the current debugging experiment. PDE observes the program from the points of view of its static structure, as specified by the source program text, and of its dynamic activity, as generated by the program execution.

The static program structure is observed by means of the PDE naming rules. A salient feature of these rules is that they make it possible to identify every program entity, independently of the point reached by the program control flow. This feature is essential to define a debugging experiment before starting up program execution, for instance.

The dynamic program activity is monitored in terms of events. An event is expressed by an access and a conditional. An *access* is the specification of a program operation, and a *conditional* is a Boolean expression whose value depends on the program state. An event occurs when the access is produced as a consequence of the activity of the target program, if the conditional is true at the time of the access.

PDE features a set of *commands* which make it possible to express *actions* in terms of manipulation of the value of the program entities, and also of the contents of the visible portion of the private storage of PDE, i.e. the PDE *registers*. Commands can be issued by the programmer at the console, interactively. Alternatively, a command can be paired with an event to form a *directive*. In this case, the directive defines a connection between this event and the actions

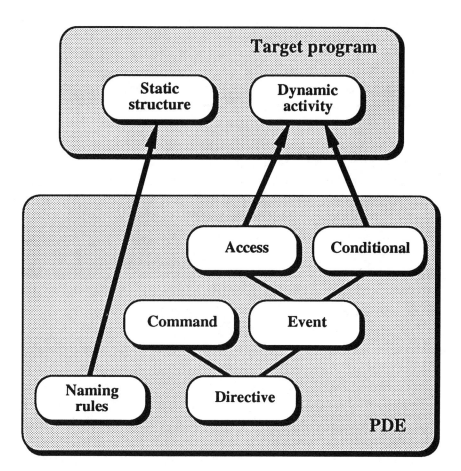

Figure 1.1 The interactions of PDE with the target program.

specified by the command. These actions will be performed on the occurrence of the event.

The activities of PDE proceed in parallel with those of the process or processes generated by the execution of the target program. It follows that the programmer can issue commands in parallel with the execution of the target program.

1.3   AN OUTLINE OF PART I

The PDE architecture, briefly introduced so far, is described in the first part of this book in detail. Chapter 2 illustrates the PDE naming rules and presents a first set of commands, including the commands to display the values of the program variables, and to assign new values to the program variables.

Chapter 3 deals with accesses, conditionals and events. It gives the rules to express an access in terms of program operations involving one or more target entities, and a conditional in terms of the value of the program variables. It also introduces the notation used to compound accesses and conditionals into events.

Chapter 4 deals with the management and utilization of the PDE registers. In addition to the *general* registers, which store partial results of the program debugging experiment, PDE maintains a collection of *special* registers, which contain information concerning the state of the target program. The commands to allocate, delete and access the registers are shown. The special registers are then used to introduce a new, simplified notation to name the target entities. In certain situations, this notation can be a useful alternative to the naming rules given in Chapter 2.

Finally, Chapter 5 completes the presentation of the PDE commands by showing the mechanisms used to group commands into command sequences, and to express selective and iterated command execution. The notation for expressing directives in terms of events and commands is illustrated, and the utilization of the directives in the definition of the layout of the program debugging experiment is shown in terms of the dynamic directive activation and termination.

Chapter 2

The target program

Objective

In this chapter, a solution to the problem of identifying the entities defined by the target program is proposed. The scope rules of the programming language, based on the *dynamic* program activity, are shown to be inadequate at the program debugging environment level. A new notation is introduced which identifies the program entities with reference to the *static* program structure.

Contents

2.1   INTRODUCTION

We will focus on high-level languages in which program statements are grouped into blocks by means of block delimiters [Pratt, 1975], [Watson, 1989]. In languages of this type, a program can be seen as a static nesting of blocks which can be represented as a tree structure, the root being the main program block. Referring to such a tree representation, we will define the *static lexical level* of a program block as the distance, i.e. the number of blocks, between that block and the root of the tree [De Prycker, 1982b].

Example 2.1

Figure 2.1 gives the program *ResMgmt*, to which reference will be made in most of the examples in this chapter. This program is written in the programming language Pascal [Jensen,1985], [Moore, 1980]. It implements a manager of pools of identical resources. The resources in a pool are numbered from 1 up to the value of the program constant *last*. A resource can be either free or busy. Three subprograms, the procedures *Init* and *Release* and the function *Get*, make it possible to use the pools. *Init* initializes the pool specified by the parameter *apool*. This procedure frees all the resources of the specified pool. *Get* makes it possible to obtain the order number of a free resource in the pool specified by the parameter *apool*. The resource is switched to the busy state. When no resource is free, 0 is returned. *Get* includes the declaration of another function called *IsBusy*, which checks the state of the resource having the order number specified by its parameter *rn* in the pool specified by its parameter *apool*. If the resource is busy, the function returns the Boolean value *true*. *IsBusy* is used in the loop in the function *Get* to check the state of the resources.

Release releases the resource with a given order number in the pool specified by the parameter *apool*. The order number is transmitted using the parameter *rn*. The corresponding resource is switched to the free state.

The program body uses a pool of resources called *rpool*. When this pool has been initialized, the resources are utilized. The variable *count* is a counter of the number of the resources obtained from the

```
program ResMgmt (...);
  label 100;
  const last = ...;
  type resnumber = 1..last;
    resnumber0 = 0..last;
    resource = (free, busy);
    respool = array [resnumber]
      of resource;
  var rpool : respool;
    res : resnumber;
    count : resnumber0;
  procedure Init (
      var apool : respool);
    var count : resnumber;
  begin {Init}
    for count := 1 to last
    do apool [count] := free
  end; {Init}
  function Get (
      var apool : respool
      ) : resnumber0;
    var count : resnumber;
    function IsBusy (
        apool : respool;
        rn : resnumber
        ) : boolean;
    begin {IsBusy}
      IsBusy := apool [rn] = busy
    end; {IsBusy}
  begin {Get}
    count := last;
    while IsBusy (apool, count)
      and (count > 1)
    do count := count - 1;
    if IsBusy (apool, count)
    then Get := 0
    else   begin
              apool [count] := busy;
              Get := count
           end
  end; {Get}
```

Figure 2.1 Pascal program *ResMgmt*.

```
                    procedure Release (
                         var apool : respool;
                         rn : resnumber);
                    begin {Release}
                       apool [rn] := free
                    end; {Release}
                    begin {ResMgmt}
                    count := 0;
                    Init (rpool);
                    ...;
                    if count < last
                    then   begin
                                 count := count + 1;
                                 res := Get (rpool)
                              end
                    else  goto 100
                    ...; {resource utilization}
                    Release (rpool, res);
                    count := count - 1;
                    ...;
                    100: ... {recovery actions}
                    end. {ResMgmt}
```

Figure 2.1 *Continued.*

pool. If a resource is needed and no free resource is available, the statement labelled 100 is executed and performs the necessary recovery actions.

Figures 2.2 and 2.3 give the block and the tree representations of the program. The tree representation shows that the static lexical level of the procedures *Init* and *Release* and of the function *Get* is 1, and that of the function *IsBusy* is 2.

2.1.1   The scope rules of the programming language

In a block-structured language, memory space is only allocated to store the value of a variable (i.e. the variable *exists*) when the program control flow reaches the block containing the declaration of that variable [De Blasi, 1990], [Maddix, 1989]. When execution of

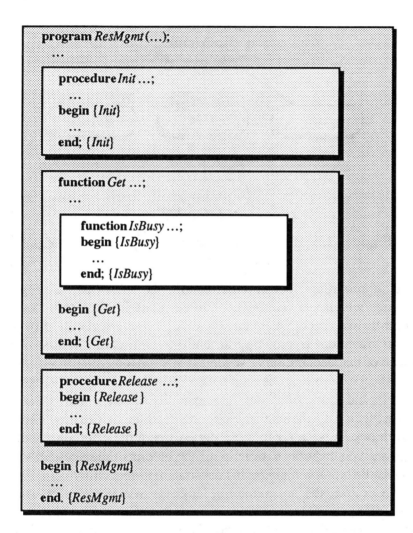

Figure 2.2 Block representation of the program *ResMgmt*.

this block terminates, the space allocated for the variable is made free. Initially, on execution of the first program statement, the only variables existing are those declared in the main program block.

Variable allocation and deallocation is only one aspect of the *scope rules* of the programming language [Findlay, 1985], [Terry, 1986]. Scope rules do not only apply to variables, but also to every other program-defined entity, e.g. statement labels, constants, types

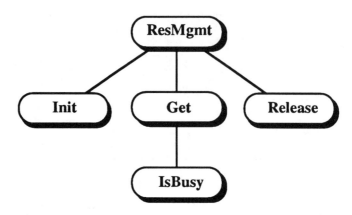

Figure 2.3 Tree representation of the program *ResMgmt*.

and subprograms. These rules identify the subset of the program entities which are *visible* (i.e. can be *named*) when the program control flow reaches a given block. A program declaration or program statement referencing an entity which is not visible in the block of that declaration or statement is erroneous.

As an example, let us refer to the Pascal programming language. The Pascal scope rules state that an entity declared in a given program block is visible in that block and in all the blocks nested within that block. If we refer to the program tree representation, we have that a given entity is visible in all the blocks in the subtree whose root is the block containing the declaration of that entity.

Of course, the programming language will not require that an identifier can be used to name a single program entity; such a constraint would, for instance, seriously limit the independent activities of programmers involved in the development of different subprograms. It follows that the language must eliminate the ambiguity which ensues if two or more entities sharing the same identifier are visible in the same block. In Pascal, this problem is solved by using the static lexical levels, as follows: let E' and E'' denote two entities declared in the blocks B' and B'', respectively, and sharing the same identifier *ID*. If both E' and E'' are visible in a block B, and *ID* is referenced in B, the reference is relevant to the entity declared in the block at the lower static lexical level distance from B. In the tree representation of the program, this means that the reference is relevant to the entity declared in the first of the blocks B' and B'' which is encountered in the path from the block B to the root of the tree. It follows that a variable may exist but not be visible from a given block. In this case, the variable cannot be named, and its value cannot be accessed.

Example 2.2

The program *ResMgmt* includes the declaration of three variables sharing the same identifier, *count*. One of these variables is declared at level 0 in the main program block. The other two variables are declared at level 1, in the procedure *Init* and the function *Get*, respectively. The variable declared in *Init* is only visible in this procedure, that declared in *Get* is visible both in *Get* and also in the function *IsBusy* declared in *Get*. The statements in *Get* which use the identifier *count* reference the variable *count* declared in *Get*. This is a consequence of the fact that the variable *count* declared in the main program block is not visible in this function.

2.1.2   The naming rules of the program debugging environment

The scope rules of the programming language are essentially aimed at restricting the operations which can be made within any given block. By limiting the consequences of erroneous statements to the visible entities, which usually are a small subset of the set of all the program entities, these rules may be especially useful in the debugging phase of program development.

On the other hand, at the PDE level, restricting the set of possible accesses to those permitted by the scope rules would, for example, prevent us from inspecting the value of a variable which is not visible from the block being executed. Of course, *accessing* a non-existent variable is always a meaningless action. However, in the PDE we must even be able to *name* non-existent entities, so that we can define a PDE experiment independently of the current state of the control flow of the target program, for instance.

Example 2.3

Let us hypothesize that PDE uses the Pascal scope rules as its own naming rules. Suppose that, in a PDE session involving the program *ResMgmt*, we have issued a directive placing a breakpoint on a statement of the function *Get* (the form of this directive will be illustrated in Chapter 5). On reaching this breakpoint, we will not be able to inspect the value of the variable *count* declared in the main program block. This is a consequence of the fact that this variable is non-visible in the function *Get*, as the identifier *count* is also used in a declaration in *Get*. Now suppose that we want to trace every access to the variable *count* declared in the function *Get*. The tracing command cannot be issued before starting up execution of *Get*, when *count* is actually allocated.

We may conclude that the scope rules of the programming language, based on a particular aspect of the *dynamic* program activity, i.e. the point reached by the control flow, are inadequate at the PDE level. Instead, PDE must have it own naming rules, and an essential requirement of these rules is that they allow us to denote every program entity. A solution is to base these rules on the *static* program structure, as specified by the source program text. In the subsequent sections, we will introduce a set of static naming rules, which will be used to denote the program entities of the different classes, i.e. blocks, variables, constants, types and statements.

2.2   BLOCKS

2.2.1   Absolute block path names

The tree representation of the target program suggests that each program block can be identified by an *absolute block path name*. This path name consists of the symbol ':' followed by a list of the identifiers of the blocks in the path from the root of the tree to that block. In this list, the symbol ':' separates the block identifiers, as follows:

:<block identifier>:<block identifier>: ... :<block identifier>

Example 2.4

In the program *ResMgmt*, the absolute path names of the main program block, of the function *Get* and of the function *IsBusy* are :*ResMgmt*, :*ResMgmt:Get*, and :*ResMgmt:Get:IsBusy*, respectively. Figure 2.4 shows portions of the program text with the addition of the absolute block path names, indicated at the left of the program statements, enclosed in curly brackets.

2.2.2   Nameless blocks

In Pascal, any program block which is not the main block is always a subprogram (a procedure or a function), and each block is associated with an identifier. Other languages, e.g. Algol [Naur, 1963], make it possible to declare a block without naming it. Nameless blocks are often used to declare new variables with a narrow scope, limited to a small portion of a subprogram, for instance.

We will indicate nameless blocks by using a self-explaining notation derived from Pascal. This notation consists of a *block statement* which takes the form of the keyword **block** followed by a

```
        {:ResMgmt}  program ResMgmt (...);
                    ...
   {:ResMgmt:Init}     procedure Init ...;
                       ...
                    end; {Init}
    {:ResMgmt:Get}   function Get ...;
                        ...
{:ResMgmt:Get:IsBusy}      function IsBusy ...;
                           ...
                       end; {IsBusy}
                    ...
                    end; {Get}
 {:ResMgmt:Release}  procedure Release ...;
                        ...
                    end; {Release}
                    ...
                    end. {ResMgmt}
```

Figure 2.4 The absolute path names of the blocks of the program *ResMgmt*.

declaration part and a statement part having the same structure as in a Pascal subprogram body:

> **block**
> ... {declaration part}
> **begin**
> ... {statement part}
> **end**

PDE denotes the nameless blocks by associating an *automatic identifier* with each of them. The automatic identifier of a given nameless block takes the form of the symbol '#' followed by an unsigned integer equal to the textual order number of that block in the block containing its declaration. By the term *textual* we intend the source program text.

Example 2.5

The program *Prog*, shown in Figure 2.5, contains the declaration of a procedure called *Proc* which includes two nameless blocks. The first of these blocks is used to declare the variable *count*, which is used to control the subsequent **for** statement. The other nameless block is used to declare the variable *temp*, which is used in the subsequent assignment statements as a temporary recipient for the exchange of the values of the variables *elem1* and *elem2*.

Figure 2.6 shows the tree representation of *Prog*. The tree has three levels, the third level being that of the two nameless blocks. The automatic identifiers of these blocks are #1 and #2, and their absolute path names are :*Prog*:*Proc*:#1 and :*Prog*:*Proc*:#2, respectively.

It should be clear that a block statement adds a new level to the tree representation of the program; whereas a compound statement only has the effect of grouping several other statements to be executed in the written order, and, therefore, does not alter the tree representation.

```
{:Prog}         program Prog (...);
                  const last = ...;
                  type elem = ...;
{:Prog:Proc}      procedure Proc (...);
                    var elem1,
                      elem2 : elem;
                    begin {Proc}
                    ...;
{:Prog:Proc:#1}     block
                      var count : 1..last;
                      begin
                      for count := 1 to last
                      do ...
                      end;
                    ...;
                    if elem1 < elem2
{:Prog:Proc:#2}     then   block
                              var temp : elem;
                            begin
                              temp := elem1;
                              elem1 := elem2;
                              elem2 := temp
                            end;
                      ...
                  end; {Proc}
                  begin {Prog}
                  ...
                  end. {Prog}
```

Figure 2.5 Program *Prog* written in a notation which makes it possible to denote nameless blocks.

Example 2.6

Figure 2.7 presents a Pascal version, called *PProg*, of the program *Prog* shown in Figure 2.5. In this version, the declarations of the variables *count* and *temp* have been grouped in the declaration part of the procedure *Proc*. A compound statement groups the assignment statements in the **then** branch of the **if** statement. Figure 2.8 shows the tree representation of *PProg*. This representation shows that this compound statement does not introduce a new level in the tree, which has a depth of two levels.

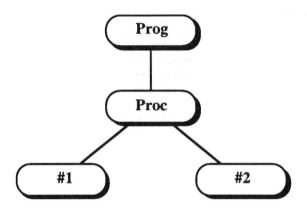

Figure 2.6 Tree representation of the program *Prog*.

2.2.3 Multiple blocks

A useful addition to the block path name notation introduced so far is a multiple-block notation for identifying several closely related blocks. For instance, suppose that we have to trace the execution of a number of nested subprograms. As will be shown in detail in Chapter 5, a PDE directive for generating traces must include the specification of the path name of every subprogram whose execution must be traced. However, specifying each path name individually could be cumbersome and error-prone. The multiple-block notation can be useful in a situation of this type.

This notation is based on the multiple block specifiers 'BLK' and 'BLKR', to be appended to a block path name. The symbol ':' separates the block path name and the multiple block specifier, as follows:

<block path name>:BLK
<block path name>:BLKR

'BLK' specifies the block denoted by the path name and all the blocks declared in this block. 'BLKR' specifies the block denoted by the path name, all the blocks declared in this block and all the blocks recursively declared in these blocks. In the program tree representation, 'BLK' denotes the block specified by the path name and all the children of this block, and 'BLKR' denotes all the blocks in the subtree whose root is the block specified by the path name.

```
{:PProg}      program PProg (...);
                const last = ...;
                type elem = ...;
{:PProg:Proc}     procedure Proc (...);
                  var elem1,
                      elem2,
                      temp : elem;
                      count : 1..last;
                  begin {Proc}
                  ...;
                  for count := 1 to last
                  do ...;
                  ...;
                  if elem1 < elem2
                  then   begin
                            temp := elem1;
                            elem1 := elem2;
                            elem2 := temp
                         end;
                  ...
                  end; {Proc}
                begin {PProg}
                ...
                end. {PProg}
```

Figure 2.7 Pascal version of the program *Prog*.

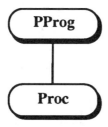

Figure 2.8 Tree representation of the program *PProg*.

Example 2.7

In the program *ResMgmt*, the path name *:ResMgmt*:BLK denotes the block *:ResMgmt* and all the blocks declared in *:ResMgmt*, i.e. the procedure *Init*, the function *Get* and the procedure *Release*. The path name *:ResMgmt*:BLKR denotes the block *:ResMgmt* and all the blocks recursively declared in *:ResMgmt*, i.e. all the program blocks.

2.2.4   Recursive subprograms

In the execution of a recursive subprogram, a new activation of the subprogram block is generated at each recursive subprogram call [Aho, 1986]. At the PDE level, the problem is to denote each one of these activations. A solution is presented here, based on an extension of the block path name notation introduced so far.

This extension maps the dynamic nature of recursive block activations into the static nature of block path names by means of an *activation specifier*, to be appended to the path name of a recursive block. This specifier takes the form of the symbol '~' followed by an unsigned integer equal to the order number of the activation, in temporal succession, the activation number 1 being the oldest. The special activation specifier '~~' denotes the most recent activation. This specifier can be omitted, as it is automatically added to every block path name not including an explicit activation specification.

Example 2.8

The program *Factorials*, shown in Figure 2.9, contains the declaration of a recursive function called *Fact* which evaluates the factorial of the value specified by its parameter *n*. The path name of the first, of the second and of the most recent activation of this function are denoted by *:Factorials:Fact~*1, *:Factorials:Fact~*2 and *:Factorials:Fact~~*, respectively. The most recent activation can also be denoted simply by *:Factorials:Fact*.

2.3   VARIABLES

In the rest of this chapter, we will use absolute block path names to identify the program entities of the different classes, i.e. variables, constants, types and statements. In this section, we will introduce a notation which can be used to identify the program variables. Of

```
{:Factorials}   program Factorials (...);
                    type nonnegint = 0..maxint;
                       posint = 1..maxint;
                    var n,
                       m,
                       i : nonnegint;
{:Factorials:Fact}  function Fact (
                          n : nonnegint
                          ) : posint;
                    begin {Fact}
                    if n = 0
                    then Fact := 1
                    else Fact := n * Fact (n - 1)
                    end; {Fact}
                    begin {Factorials}
                    readln (n, m);
                    for i := n to m
                    do writeln (i, Fact (i))
                    end. {Factorials}
```

Figure 2.9 Pascal program *Factorials*.

course, this notation is an essential PDE feature, which is likely to be used in almost every PDE experiment to inspect the partial results of the computation as well as to keep track of the causes of the evolution of the control flow, for instance.

PDE identifies a variable declared in a given block by means of the path name of this block and the variable identifier, separated by the symbol ':', as follows:

    <block path name>:<variable identifier>

Example 2.9

In the program *ResMgmt*, the variable *count* declared in the main program block is denoted by *:ResMgmt:count*, and the variable *count* declared in the function *Get* is denoted by *:Res-Mgmt:Get:count*. Figure 2.10 shows portions of the program text, to which the names of the variables have been added.

This variable-naming notation is based on the static, textual structure of the target program rather than on the dynamic program

```
                              program ResMgmt (...);
                              ...
        {:ResMgmt:rpool}      var rpool : respool;
          {:ResMgmt:res}        res : resnumber;
        {:ResMgmt:count}        count : resnumber0;
                              procedure Init ...;
     {:ResMgmt:Init:count}      var count : resnumber;

                              end; {Init}
                              function Get ...;
     {:ResMgmt:Get:count}       var count : resnumber;
                                function IsBusy ...;

                                end; {IsBusy}
                              ...
                              end; {Get}
                              procedure Release ...;

                              end; {Release}
                              ...
                              end. {ResMgmt}
```

Figure 2.10   The names used by PDE to identify the variables of the program *ResMgmt*.

activity. By univocally identifying the block to which any given variable belongs, the variable is given a name which is unique for the whole target program. In this way, the notation satisfies the requirements for the naming rules of PDE, which we have identified in Section 2.1. Each variable is named independently of the point reached by the program control flow and of the storage allocation and deallocation activities connected with execution of the program. It can be used to name non-visible as well as non-existent variables, thereby solving the problems originated by several variables declared in different blocks and sharing the same identifier.

2.3.1   Subprogram parameters

The PDE naming rules assimilate the parameters of a given subprogram to the local variables of that subprogram. It follows that a parameter is identified by means of the block path name of the subprogram and the formal parameter identifier, separated by the symbol ':', as follows:

<block path name>:<formal parameter identifier>

The result of a function is identified by the block path name of the function and the function identifier, separated by the symbol ':', as follows:

<block path name>:<function identifier>

Example 2.10

In the program *ResMgmt*, the parameter *apool* of the function *Get* is denoted by *:ResMgmt:Get:apool*, and the result of this function is denoted by *:ResMgmt:Get:Get*. Figure 2.11 shows portions of the program text, with the addition of the names of the subprogram parameters.

2.3.2   Multiple variables

A useful addition to the variable naming rules introduced so far is a multiple variable notation for identifying several closely related variables. For instance, suppose that we want to display the values of the variables declared in a given subprogram. As will be shown in detail in Section 2.7, a PDE output command must include the name of every entity whose value is to be displayed. The multiple variable notation allows us to obtain this result without having to specify the name of each variable individually (a similar PDE feature has been illustrated in Section 2.2 with respect to multiple blocks).

This notation consists of the multiple variable specifier 'VAR'. If appended to the path name of a block, as follows:

<block path name>:VAR

the multiple variable specifier denotes all the variables declared in the block.

An interesting application of the multiple variable specifier 'VAR' is its joint utilization with the multiple block specifiers 'BLK' and 'BLKR', introduced in Section 2.2. An example of this application is shown below.

```
                                       program ResMgmt (...);
                                       ...
                                       procedure Init (
{:ResMgmt:Init:apool}                      var apool : respool);
                                       ...
                                       end; {Init}
                                       function Get (
{:ResMgmt:Get:apool}                       var apool : respool
{:ResMgmt:Get:Get}                         ) : resnumber0;
                                       ...
                                       function IsBusy (
{:ResMgmt:Get:IsBusy:apool}                apool : respool;
{:ResMgmt:Get:IsBusy:rn}                   rn : resnumber
{:ResMgmt:Get:IsBusy:IsBusy}               ) : boolean;
                                       ...
                                       end; {IsBusy}
                                       ...
                                       end; {Get}
                                       procedure Release (
{:ResMgmt:Release:apool}                   var apool : respool;
{:ResMgmt:Release:rn}                      rn : resnumber);
                                       ...
                                       end; {Release}
                                       ...
                                       end. {ResMgmt}
```

Figure 2.11   The names used by PDE to identify the parameters of the subprograms of the program *ResMgmt*.

Example 2.11

In the program *ResMgmt*, :*ResMgmt:Get:*VAR denotes the variable *count* declared in the function *Get*, the function parameter :*ResMgmt:Get:apool* and the function result :*ResMgmt:Get:Get*. :*ResMgmt:*VAR denotes all the variables declared in the main program block, i.e. the variables :*ResMgmt:rpool*, :*ResMgmt:res* and :*ResMgmt:count*. :*ResMgmt:*BLKR:VAR denotes all the variables declared in the blocks :*ResMgmt:*BLKR, i.e. all the program variables.

2.4   CONSTANTS

The introduction of constants in a program generally facilitates program development [Koffman, 1986]. By associating an identifier with a value, constants increase program readability. If different instances of a given value are used in different program portions, it is far easier to discover the relationships between these instances if an identifier is used as a substitute for the value itself.

Constants also enhance program modifiability. If a program value is specified in terms of a constant, then we can modify this value by simply modifying the constant declaration, otherwise we have to modify all the program declarations and statements which depend on this value. This is not only hard work, but is also prone to errors, especially in a large program, where the probability that one of the required changes is forgotten is high.

Example 2.12

In the program *ResMgmt*, the constant *last* defined in the main program block is used in the declaration of the type *resnumber*, for instance. This constant is then used in the **for** statement in the function *Init* to specify the upper bound for the variable *count*. An inspection of the program evidences the close relationship between this upper bound and the number of the elements in the array *rpool*, expressed in terms of the type *resnumber*. It is likely that this relationship is not so evident if we replace the identifier of the constant with its actual value.

Now, let us suppose that we have to double the size of the pools of resources. In the program in the present form, this modification can be simply accomplished by changing the value of the constant *last*. If the program were written without using constants, we would have to modify both the declaration of the type *resnumber* and the upper bound of the **for** statement in the function *Init*.

PDE identifies a constant by using a notation similar to that used for variables, i.e. the path name of the block containing the constant declaration and the constant identifier, separated by the symbol ':', as follows:

<block path name>:<constant identifier>

Example 2.13

In the program *ResMgmt*, *:ResMgmt:last* denotes the constant *last* declared in the main program block.

We also have a multiple constant notation consisting of the multiple constant specifier 'CONST'. If appended to the path name of a block, as follows:

<block path name>:CONST

the multiple constant specifier denotes all the constants declared in that block. 'CONST' can also be used together with the multiple block specifiers 'BLK' and 'BLKR', introduced in Section 2.2, to denote all the constants declared in multiple blocks.

2.5   TYPES

A *data type* is the specification of a set of values and the set of possible operations on these values [Sommerville, 1989]. A variable of a given type can only assume values of that type. High-level languages feature a set of built-in types, which are part of the language. In Pascal, the built-in types are the scalar types *integer*, *real*, *boolean* and *char*. For instance, the values of the type *boolean* are *false* and *true*, and the operations which can be performed on these values include the Boolean operations **and, or, not**.

Of course, the set of the built-in types will probably not be appropriate for every possible application. However, the introduction of additional built-in types tends to increase the complexity of the language noticeably, while enhancing its expressive power only marginally. In a different approach, the language will feature a set of mechanisms for the definition of *abstract data types* [Feldman, 1988], [Ghezzi, 1987], [Guttag, 1977], [Lopriore, 1984]. The programmer will use these mechanisms to define the type abstractions which are required for the application he intends to write, thereby mapping the domain of the problem into the domain of the language [Fairley, 1985].

In Pascal, a new scalar type can be defined by *enumeration*, i.e. declaring the identifiers of the values of the new type and an ordering relation among these values, and by specifying a *subrange*, which is a subset of the set of the values of another scalar type. By limiting the range of the permitted variable values, subranges increase the probability that an erroneous assignment generates a runtime error, thereby facilitating program debugging. By allowing the programmer to associate meaningful identifiers with data values, enumerated types increase program readability.

Pascal also features a set of *aggregate constructors*, which make it possible to define composite types in terms of other scalar or composite types. Examples are the *array* type constructor, which aggregates values which are all of the same type, and the *record* type constructor, which aggregates values of possibly different types [Toy, 1986]. The programmer will use these type-definition mechanisms to give support to the internal representation of his abstract data types. The operations of a type will be concretized by means of subprograms whose parameters will include variables of that type.

Example 2.14

The program *ResMgmt* defines the abstract data type *respool*. As seen in Example 2.1, a variable of this type implements a pool of identical resources. The values which the variable can assume are the possible sets of the states (*free* or *busy*) of these resources. The operations of *respool* make it possible to initialize a pool, to obtain the order number of a free resource in a given pool, and to release a resource having a given order number in a given pool. These operations are implemented by the subprograms *Init*, *Get* and *Release*, respectively.

Unfortunately, Pascal features no mechanism to prevent the internal representation of a variable of a given abstract type being accessed without executing the subprograms implementing the operations of that type. Other languages, e.g. Concurrent Pascal [Brinch Hansen, 1975], Euclid [Lampson, 1977], Edison [Brinch Hansen,

1981], Ada [ANSI, 1983], Modula-2 [Wirth, 1988a], and Oberon [Wirth, 1988b], allow the programmer to enforce a real encapsulation of abstract types. In these languages, the only way of accessing the internal representation of a variable is by using the operations of its type.

The importance in program development of language constructs for the definition of data abstractions has been widely demonstrated [Feldman, 1981], [Ghezzi, 1987], [Sommerville, 1989]. By hiding implementation details, these constructs make it possible to change the internal representation of a type without having to change the program modules using that type. Abstract data types are especially useful in the development of large programs. In particular, they strongly support the *bottom-up* programming methodology [Shooman, 1983], [Terry, 1987]. In this methodology, a large program is partitioned into program layers organized hierarchically. Essentially, a layer consists of a set of abstract data types, which are concretized by using the types defined by the underlying layers. Program development proceeds from the lowest layers to higher layers. This helps to isolate programming errors. If a difference is detected between intended and actual program behaviour while debugging a given layer, the error is localized in the abstract data types which form that layer.

In PDE, referencing a type means referencing any variable of that type. PDE identifies a type by means of the path name of the block containing the declaration of that type and the type identifier, separated by the symbol ':', as follows:

<block path name>:<type identifier>

Example 2.15

In the program *ResMgmt*, :*ResMgmt*:*respool* denotes the type *respool* declared in the main program block. By referencing this type, we reference all the variables of this type, i.e. the variable *rpool* declared in the main program block, and the parameter *apool* of the functions *Get* and *IsBusy*, and of the procedures *Release* and *Init*. Figure 2.12 shows portions of the program text, with the addition of the names of the program types.

```
                              program ResMgmt (...);
                              ...
{:ResMgmt:resnumber}          type resnumber = 1..last;
{:ResMgmt:resnumber0}            resnumber0 = 0..last;
{:ResMgmt:resource}              resource = (free, busy);
{:ResMgmt:respool}               respool = array [resnumber]
                                   of resource;
                              ...
                              procedure Init ...;
                                 ...
                              end; {Init}
                              function Get ...;
                                 ...
                                 function IsBusy ...;
                                    ...
                                 end; {IsBusy}
                                 ...
                              end; {Get}
                              procedure Release ...;
                                 ...
                              end; {Release}
                              ...
                              end. {ResMgmt}
```

Figure 2.12   The names used by PDE to identify the types of the program *ResMgmt*.

We also have a multiple-type notation consisting of the multiple type specifier 'TYPE'. If appended to the path name of a block, as follows:

    <block path name>:TYPE

the multiple type specifier denotes all the types declared in that block.

2.6   STATEMENTS

A program statement may or may not have a user-defined label. PDE identifies a labelled statement by means of the path name of the block enclosing that statement and the statement label, separated by the symbol '@', as follows:

<block path name>@<statement label>

PDE associates automatic labels with the unlabelled statements. The automatic label of a statement of a given block consists of the symbol '$' followed by an unsigned integer, equal to the textual order number of the statement in that block. The special automatic label '$$' denotes the last statement of the specified block. A symbol '@' separating a block path name and an automatic statement label can be omitted.

Example 2.16

The program *ResMgmt* features a single labelled statement, which is enclosed in the main program body. The label of this statement is 100, and this statement therefore will be denoted by *:ResMgmt@*100. All the other statements will be denoted by using automatic labels. For instance, the automatic label of the first statement of the function *Get* (a **begin-end** statement) is $1, thus this statement is denoted by *:ResMgmt:Get@*$1 or (in abbreviated form) *:ResMgmt:Get*$1. The second and last statement of *Get* (which are both assignment statements) are denoted by *:ResMgmt:Get*$2 and *:ResMgmt:Get*$9, respectively. The last statement can be also denoted by *:ResMgmt:Get*$$. Figure 2.13 shows the program *ResMgmt*, with the addition of the names of all the program entities. In this figure, for simplicity, the block path name is only indicated in the first statement of each block.

2.6.1 Multiple statements

The multiple statement notation is based on the multiple statement specifiers '*' and '**', to be appended to the name of a statement, as follows:

<statement name>*
<statement name>**

If the named statement is a structured statement, '*' denotes this statement and all its component statements, and '**' denotes the

```
      {:ResMgmt}   program ResMgmt (...);
                   label 100;
 {:ResMgmt:last}   const last = ...;
{:ResMgmt:resnumber}   type resnumber = 1..last;
{:ResMgmt:resnumber0}       resnumber0 = 0..last;
{:ResMgmt:resource}         resource = (free, busy);
 {:ResMgmt:respool}         respool = array [resnumber]
                               of resource;
   {:ResMgmt:rpool}   var rpool : respool;
     {:ResMgmt:res}       res : resnumber;
   {:ResMgmt:count}       count : resnumber0;
    {:ResMgmt:Init}   procedure Init (
{:ResMgmt:Init:apool}       var apool : respool);
{:ResMgmt:Init:count}       var count : resnumber;
 {:ResMgmt:Init$1}   begin {Init}
           {$2}         for count := 1 to last
           {$3}         do apool [count] := free
                     end; {Init}

     {:ResMgmt:Get}   function Get (
{:ResMgmt:Get:apool}       var apool : respool
   {:ResMgmt:Get:Get}       ) : resnumber0;
{:ResMgmt:Get:count}       var count : resnumber;
{:ResMgmt:Get:IsBusy}       function IsBusy (
{:ResMgmt:Get:IsBusy:apool}       apool : respool;
{:ResMgmt:Get:IsBusy:rn}       rn : resnumber
{:ResMgmt:Get:IsBusy:IsBusy}       ) : boolean;
{:ResMgmt:Get:IsBusy$1}       begin {IsBusy}
           {$2}         IsBusy := apool [rn] = busy
                     end; {IsBusy}

{:ResMgmt:Get$1}   begin {Get}
           {$2}     count := last;
           {$3}     while IsBusy (apool, count)
                       and (count > 1)
           {$4}     do count := count - 1;
           {$5}     if IsBusy (apool, count)
           {$6}     then Get := 0
           {$7}     else   begin
           {$8}             apool [count] := busy;
           {$9}             Get := count
                           end
                   end; {Get}
```

Figure 2.13 The names used by PDE to identify the entities which form the program *ResMgmt*.

```
          {:ResMgmt:Release}      procedure Release (
     {:ResMgmt:Release:apool}          var apool : respool;
        {:ResMgmt:Release:rn}          rn : resnumber);
        {:ResMgmt:Release$1}      begin {Release}
                        {$2}          apool [rn] := free
                                  end; {Release}
          {:ResMgmt$1}  begin {ResMgmt}
                        {$2}          count := 0;
                        {$3}          Init (rpool);
                        {$4}          ...;
                        {$5}          if count < last
                        {$6}          then  begin
                        {$7}                  count := count + 1;
                        {$8}                  res := Get (rpool)
                                            end
                        {$9}          else  goto 100
                       {$10}          ...; {resource utilization}
                       {$11}          Release (rpool, res);
                       {$12}          count := count - 1;
                       {$...}          ...;
                     {@100}  100: ... {recovery actions}
                                  end. {ResMgmt}
```

Figure 2.13   *Continued.*

named statement, all its component statements and all the components of these statements, recursively. If the named statement is a simple statement, '*' and '**' have no effect.

Example 2.17

In the program *ResMgmt*, *:ResMgmt:Get*$1* denotes the statement *:ResMgmt:Get*$1 (the body of the function *Get*) and its component statements *:ResMgmt:Get*$2, *:ResMgmt:Get*$3 and *:ResMgmt:Get*$5. *:ResMgmt:Get*$1** denotes the statement *:ResMgmt:Get*$1 and all the statements which recursively compound this statement, i.e. all the statements of the function *Get*.

The multiple statement notation is based on the *static* structure of the source program. Consequently, if we apply this notation to a given structured statement, and a component of this statement causes the program control flow to reach other statements which, however, are not part of this structured statement, these other statements are *not* included in the multiple statement. This result can actually be obtained by using a *dynamic* statement specification technique (applications of this technique will be illustrated in Chapter 6). This important point is illustrated by the following example.

Example 2.18

In the program *ResMgmt*, *:ResMgmt:Get*$1** denotes all the statements of the function *Get*. However, it *does not* denote the statements which form the function *IsBusy* called by the statements *:ResMgmt:Get*$3 and *:ResMgmt:Get*$5.

2.7   ACCESSING THE PROGRAM ENTITIES

2.7.1   Assigning a value to a program variable

A new value can be assigned to a program variable using the **set** command, which is as follows:

> **set** <variable name> **to** <program expression>

Execution of this command evaluates the program expression and assigns the result to the named variable. The variable and the value of the expression must be of the same type. The factors of the expression can be program variables, program constants, program enumeration literals, character literals, numeric literals and string literals.

Example 2.19

In the program *ResMgmt*, the command

> **set** *:ResMgmt:count* **to** *:ResMgmt:last*

replaces the value of the variable *count* declared in the main program block with the value of the constant *last* declared in this block. This action can be used, for instance, to check the behaviour of the program in a situation in which no free resources are available.

The implementation may restrict the applicability of the **set** command, for example, to the most recent activation of each variable [Elliot, 1982], or even to the variables in the block containing the statement being executed. Furthermore, the implementation may explicitly state that the values of the program variables will be retrieved and changed in memory. In this case, if the value of a variable is stored in a register of the central processor, the effects of a **set** command involving this variable may not be reflected by later use of the variable.

2.7.2   Input and output

Input and output operations involving the values of the program variables can be performed by means of the **get** and the **put** commands. The **get** command has the form

> **get** <variable name> , ... , <variable name> **from** <file>

For each named variable, this command reads a sequence of characters from the specified file, converts this sequence into a value of the same type as the variable, and assigns this value to the variable. The file specification can be omitted. In this case, the keyword **from** must also be omitted, and the character sequences are received from the console. The implementation may restrict the applicability of the **get** command, and the possible restrictions include those discussed previously for the **set** command.

Example 2.20

In the program *ResMgmt*, the command

> **get** *:ResMgmt:count* **from** INFILE

replaces the value of the variable *count* declared in the main program block with quantities taken from the file INFILE.

The **put** command has the form

> **put** <program expression> , ... , <program expression> **to**
> <file>

This command interprets the value of each program expression according to its type, and converts this value into a sequence of characters. The contents of the specified file are replaced with these sequences. If the file does not exist, it is created. The file specification can be omitted. In this case, the keyword **to** must also be omitted, and the character sequences are transmitted to the console.

Output can be appended to a file by specifying the **append** attribute in the **put** command, as follows:

> **put** <program expression> , ... , <program expression> **append to** <file>

Example 2.21

In the program *ResMgmt*, the command

> **put** 'Busy resources: ', :*ResMgmt:count* **to** OUTFILE

replaces the contents of the file OUTFILE with a string literal and the value of the variable *count* declared in the main program block. The string literal is used to insert a comment in the output, for increased readability.

The command

> **put** 'Busy resources: ', :*ResMgmt:count* **append to** OUT-
> FILE

appends the output to the file OUTFILE.

2.7.3   Input and output redirection

The parameters of the **get** and the **put** commands include the name of the file which must be used for the input or output operation. We will now introduce a mechanism which can be used to permanently redirect the data input or output from/to a given file. This mechanism takes the form of the **permanent input** and the **permanent**

output commands. The **permanent input** command is as follows:

permanent input <file>

It causes the specified file to be used by every subsequent input command not featuring an explicit specification of the input file. The console can be resumed for data input by issuing the command

permanent input CONSOLE

The **permanent output** command is as follows:

permanent output <file>

It causes the specified file to be used by every subsequent output command not featuring an explicit specification of the output file. The console can be resumed for data output by issuing the command

permanent output CONSOLE

By eliminating the need to specify the file name explicitly in each input and output command, permanent input and output redirection is especially useful in a program debugging experiment using the same file for several input or output commands, for example, a program tracing experiment using a single trace file.

Example 2.22

The command

permanent output OUTFILE

causes the data output generated by every subsequent output command to be sent to the file OUTFILE. In a PDE session involving the program *ResMgmt*, if we now issue the command

put *:ResMgmt:count* **append**

the value of the variable *count* declared in the main program block will be appended to OUTFILE.

2.8   ALIASING BLOCK PATH NAMES

As seen in Sections 2.1 and 2.2, a given identifier can be used in more than one program declaration to denote different target entities, and block path names are used at PDE level to discriminate between these entities. On the other hand, specifying a full path name for every entity may represent a heavy typing burden, especially for deeply nested blocks identified by long path names. We will now introduce a mechanism which allows the programmer to define short, easy-to-type aliases for complex path names. This mechanism takes the form of a PDE command, the **alias** command, which is as follows:

>   **alias** <alias identifier> := <block path name>

This command defines an alias for the specified block path name. The alias identifier can be used as a substitute for the block path name it represents, and is just an abbreviation for the path name. The command

>   **alias display to** <file>

produces a display of all active aliases in the form of a sequence of characters. The contents of the specified file are replaced with this sequence. If the file does not exist, it is created. The file specification can be omitted. In this case, the keyword **to** must also be omitted, and the character sequence is transmitted to the console.

An alias display can be appended to a file by issuing an **alias display** command with the **append** attribute, as follows:

>   **alias display append to** <file>

A permanent redirection to a given file of the data output generated by the **alias display** command can be obtained by means of the **permanent output** command, introduced in Section 2.7.

The command

>   **unalias** <alias identifier>, <alias identifier>, ..., <alias identifier>

removes the aliases with the given identifiers. Finally, the command

>   **unalias all**

removes all active aliases.

Example 2.23

The command

> **alias** *Get* := :*ResMgmt*:*Get*

causes *Get* to be an alias for the block path name :*ResMgmt*:*Get*. The variable *count* declared in the function *Get* can now be simply denoted by *Get*:*count*, and the first statement of this function can be denoted by *Get*$1.

Chapter 3

Accesses, conditionals, events

Objective

The objective of this chapter is to introduce a set of mechanisms which make it possible to monitor the activity of the target program from the viewpoints of the operations performed by the program and the evolution of the program state.

Contents

In the previous chapter, we considered the *static* structure of the target program, and we introduced the naming rules used by PDE to denote the program-defined entities. In this chapter, we will consider the *dynamic* activity of the target program. We will introduce a set of mechanisms which allow us to observe this activity by expressing *accesses* in terms of the program operations, *conditionals* in terms of the program state, and *events* in terms of accesses and conditionals.

3.1   ACCESSES

An *access* is the specification of an operation occurring as a consequence of the execution of the target program. Accesses can be elementary or multiple. An *elementary access* is the specification of the name of a program entity and an *access mode*. The name of the entity will be specified by using the naming rules introduced in Chapter 2. The symbol '!' separates the entity name and the access mode, as follows:

> <entity name>!<access mode>

For each class of program entities, i.e. variables, constants, types and statements, a set of access modes is defined, and each mode corresponds to a subset of the set of the operations which can be performed on an entity of that class. The specification of the access mode can be omitted. In this case, the symbol '!' must also be omitted, the access assumes the form of an entity name, and a default access mode is used.

Later in this section, we will introduce the access modes for each class of program entities, and, for each mode, we will analyse the meaning of an elementary access expressed in terms of that mode with respect to the activity of the target program. A *program cycle* is any aspect of the execution of the target program which causes an operation to be performed on a program entity. At any given program cycle, a given elementary access is *produced* if the mode of the operation performed at that cycle and the program entity involved in that operation match the specification of that elementary access.

A *multiple access* is the specification of two or more elementary accesses, separated by the symbol ',' as follows:

> <elementary access> , <elementary access> , ... , <elementary access>

At any given program cycle, a given multiple access will be produced if at least one of the elementary accesses which form that multiple access is produced at that cycle.

Let A_1 and A_2 be two elementary or multiple accesses. A_1 is *equivalent* to A_2 if they both are produced at the same program cycles, i.e. A_1 is produced at every program cycle at which A_2 is produced, and A_2 is produced at every program cycle at which A_1 is produced.

3.1.1   Variables

Programming languages allow the programmer to declare not only *simple* variables to store a single quantity of a given type, e.g. integers and booleans, but also *structured* variables, e.g. arrays and records, for the storage of collections of component values of other simple or structured types [Ghezzi, 1987]. Two operations are possible on a simple variable: read the value of the variable; write a new value into the variable. Three access modes are defined for a simple variable, *read*, *write* and *read/write*. In the specification of an elementary access, these modes are denoted by the symbols 'R', 'W' and 'RW', respectively. A read-mode elementary access to a given simple variable is produced by any read operation, a write-mode elementary access by any write operation, and a read/write-mode elementary access by any read or write operation involving that variable. It follows that a read/write-mode elementary access to a given simple variable is equivalent to a multiple access expressed in terms of two elementary accesses to that variable, one in read mode and the other in write mode.

The read mode is the default simple variable access mode. Therefore, if the access mode is omitted in the specification of an elementary access to a variable, the read mode is used.

Example 3.1

Figure 3.1 shows the Pascal program *IntArrays*. This program defines an array type called *intarrtype*, which is a collection of integer elements numbered from 1 to the value of the constant *maxitem*. The procedure *Rotate* rotates the elements of the array transmitted by its input parameter *circular* by replacing the value of the ith element with the value of the $(i-1)$th element. This procedure treats the array as a circular array, considering the last element as adjacent to the first. The variable *lastelem* is used to hold the value of the last element, which will be assigned to the first element at the end of the

```
{:IntArrays}              program IntArrays (...);
{:IntArrays:maxitem}        const maxitem = ...;
{:IntArrays:index}          type index = 1..maxitem;
{:IntArrays:intarrtype}       intarrtype = array [index] of integer;
{:IntArrays:intarr}         var intarr : intarrtype;
{:IntArrays:Rotate}         procedure Rotate (
{:IntArrays:Rotate:circular}      var circular : intarrtype);
{:IntArrays:Rotate:position}      var position : 2..maxitem;
{:IntArrays:Rotate:lastelem}      lastelem : integer;
{:IntArrays:Rotate$1}       begin {Rotate}
{$2}                        lastelem := circular [maxitem];
{$3}                        for position := maxitem downto 2
{$4}                        do circular [position] :=
                                circular [position-1];
{$5}                        circular [1] := lastelem
                          end; {Rotate}
{:IntArrays$1}            begin {IntArrays}
{$2}                        ...;
{$3}                        Rotate (intarr);
{$...}                      ...
                          end. {IntArrays}
```

Figure 3.1 Pascal program *IntArrays*.

rotation. All the other array elements are processed by a **for** statement, which uses the variable *position* to select the element to be processed by the current iteration.

In the program *IntArrays*, *:IntArrays:Rotate:lastelem*!R, *:IntArrays:Rotate:lastelem*!W and *:IntArrays:Rotate:lastelem*!RW denote a read-, a write- and a read/write-mode elementary access to the variable *lastelem*, respectively. By using the default variable access mode, the first of these accesses can be simply denoted by *:IntArrays:Rotate:lastelem*. The elementary access *:IntArrays:Rotate:lastelem*!RW is equivalent to the multiple access

:IntArrays:Rotate:lastelem!R, *:IntArrays:Rotate:lastelem*!W

The statement *:IntArrays:Rotate*$2 produces a *:IntArrays:Rotate:lastelem*!W access, and the statement *:IntArrays:Rotate*$5 produces a *:IntArrays:Rotate:lastelem*!R access. Both these statements produce a *:IntArrays:Rotate:lastelem*!RW access.

An elementary access in a given mode to a structured variable is equivalent to a multiple access expressed in terms of an elementary access for each of the components of that structured variable. The mode of each of these elementary accesses is that of the structured variable access.

Example 3.2

In the program *IntArrays*, *:IntArrays:Rotate:circular*!RW is a read/write-mode elementary access to the parameter *circular* of the procedure *Rotate*. This parameter has the array type *intarrtype*. The access is equivalent to the multiple access

> *:IntArrays:Rotate:circular*[1]!RW, *:IntArrays:Rotate:circular*[2]!RW, ..., *:IntArrays:Rotate:circular*[*:IntArrays:maxitem*]!RW

expressed in terms of a read/write-mode elementary access to each of the elements of the array. This access is produced twice on each iteration of the **for** statement *:IntArrays:Rotate*$3, as a consequence of the read-mode access and the write-mode access to the array which are produced by the execution of the assignment statement *:IntArrays:Rotate*$4.

In Section 2.3, we introduced a multiple variable notation for identifying several closely-related variables. An elementary access in a given mode to a multiple variable is equivalent to a multiple access expressed in terms of an elementary access for each of the components of that multiple variable. The mode of each of these elementary accesses is that of the multiple variable access.

Example 3.3

In the program *IntArrays*, the read-mode elementary access *:IntArrays:Rotate*:VAR!R to the multiple variable *:IntArrays:Rotate*:VAR is equivalent to the multiple access

> *:IntArrays:Rotate:circular*!R, *:IntArrays:Rotate:position*!R, *:IntArrays:Rotate:lastelem*!R

expressed in terms of read-mode elementary accesses to the parameter *circular* of the procedure *Rotate* and to the variables *position* and *lastelem* declared in this procedure.

An elementary access to a given variable is always produced *after* performing the target program operation involving that variable. For a write-mode access, this means that any elaboration performed by PDE as a consequence of the access and involving the contents of that variable will use the value assigned to the variable by the write.

Example 3.4

In the execution of the program *IntArrays*, the write-mode elementary access :*IntArrays:Rotate:lastelem*!W to the variable *lastelem* declared in the procedure *Rotate* is produced by the assignment statement :*IntArrays:Rotate*$2. Suppose that we have issued a directive causing PDE to display the contents of *lastelem* when this access is produced (the form of this directive will be illustrated in Chapter 5). On execution of the statement :*IntArrays:Rotate*$2, PDE will display the value of the last element of the array, which is assigned to *lastelem* by this statement.

3.1.2   Constants

A single operation is possible on a constant, i.e. read its value. This operation corresponds to the access mode *read*. In the specification of an elementary access to a constant, this access mode is denoted by the symbol 'R' and can be omitted.

Example 3.5

In the program *IntArrays*, :*IntArrays:maxitem*!R is a read-mode elementary access to the constant *maxitem* defined in the main program block. This access can be simply denoted by :*IntArrays:maxitem*. In the execution of the procedure *Rotate*, this access is produced, for instance, by the assignment statement :*IntArrays:Rotate*$2 while selecting the last element of the array *circular*.

An elementary access to a structured or multiple constant is equivalent to a multiple access expressed in terms of an elementary access for each of the components of that structured or multiple constant, and the mode of each of these elementary accesses is that of the structured or multiple constant access.

3.1.3 Types

As seen in Section 2.5, in PDE referencing a type means referencing any variable of this type. It follows that the operations valid for variables are also valid for types, i.e. read and write operations, and the type access modes are *read* ('R'), *write* ('W') and *read/write* ('RW'). The read mode is the default mode. An elementary access to a given type in a given access mode is produced by any operation performed in that mode, which involves a variable of that type. It follows that an elementary access to a given type is equivalent to a multiple access expressed in terms of an elementary access for each variable of that type, and the mode of each of these variable accesses is that of the type access.

Example 3.6

In the program *IntArrays*, *:IntArrays:intarrtype*!R is a read-mode elementary access to the type *intarrtype* declared in the main program block. This access is equivalent to the multiple access

   :IntArrays:intarr!R, *:IntArrays:Rotate:circular*!R

expressed in terms of the read-mode elementary accesses to the variable *intarr* declared in the main program block and the parameter *circular* of the procedure *Rotate*, both of the type *intarrtype*. In the execution of *Rotate*, this type access is produced, for instance, by the assignment statement *:IntArrays:Rotate*$2, which performs a read operation on an element of *circular*.

An elementary access in a given mode to a multiple type is equivalent to a multiple access expressed in terms of an elementary access for each of the components of that multiple type. The mode of each of these elementary accesses is that of the multiple type access.

3.1.4 Statements

Programming languages allow the programmer to group *simple* statements expressing elementary program activities into *structured* statements expressing composite activities in terms of other simple or structured statements. In Pascal, examples of simple statements are the assignment statement and the **goto** statement, and examples of structured statements are the **begin-end** statement, the **if** statement and the **while** statement. Two operations are possible on a simple or structured statement: begin and terminate the execution of this statement. These operations correspond to the access modes *begin* and *terminate*, respectively. In the specification of an elementary access, these modes are denoted by the symbols 'B' and 'T', respectively. A begin-mode elementary access to a given statement is produced by the beginning of the activities involved in the execution of this statement, and a terminate-mode elementary access is produced by the completion of these activities. The begin mode is the default mode.

Example 3.7

In the program *IntArrays*, *:IntArrays:Rotate*$3!B and *:IntArrays:Rotate*$3!T denote a begin-mode elementary access and a terminate-mode elementary access to the **for** statement *:IntArrays:Rotate*$3. By taking advantage of the default statement access mode, the access *:IntArrays:Rotate*$3!B can be simply denoted by *:IntArrays:Rotate*$3. This access is produced by the beginning of the activities involved in the execution of the **for** statement, before starting up the first iteration. It is equivalent to the terminate-mode elementary access *:IntArrays:Rotate*$2!T to the assignment statement *:IntArrays:Rotate*$2. The access *:IntArrays:Rotate*$3!T is produced by the completion of the activities involved in the execution of the **for** statement, after terminating the last iteration. It is equivalent to the begin-mode elementary access *:IntArrays:Rotate*$5!B to the assignment statement *:IntArrays:Rotate*$5.

:*IntArrays:Rotate*$1!B and :*IntArrays:Rotate*$1!T denote a begin-mode elementary access and a terminate-mode elementary access to the first statement of the procedure *Rotate*, i.e. the **begin-end** statement which forms the procedure body. These accesses are produced by the beginning and by the completion of the activities involved in the execution of the procedure.

When analysing program behaviour, it can be useful to define a dynamic ordering of the statements, as follows:

Definition 3.1. The statement S' *dynamically precedes* the statement S if the beginning of the activities involved in the execution of S' precedes the beginning of the activities involved in the execution of S.

Definition 3.2. The statement S'' *dynamically follows* the statement S if the completion of the activities involved in the execution of S'' follows the completion of the activities involved in the execution of S.

Of course, as a consequence of modifications to the control flow due to the execution of control structures such as selection statements and repetition statements, the static ordering of the statements, specified by the source program text, may not coincide with the dynamic ordering.

It should be noted that, dynamically, a given statement may both precede and follow another given statement. This is the case, for instance, for a structured statement with respect to anyone of its component statements. In the following example, this aspect of program dynamics is considered from the point of view of the statement accesses.

Example 3.8

In the execution of the procedure *Rotate* in the program *IntArrays*, the begin-mode elementary access :*IntArrays:Rotate*$1!B to the **begin-end** statement :*IntArrays:Rotate*$1 which forms the procedure body precedes the begin-mode elementary access :*IntArrays:Rotate*$2!B to the assignment statement :*IntArrays:Rotate*$2, and the terminate-mode elementary access :*IntArrays:Rotate*$1!T follows the terminate-mode elementary access *:IntArrays:Rotate*$2!T.

The begin-mode elementary access *:IntArrays:Rotate*$3!B to the **for** statement *:IntArrays:Rotate*$3 precedes every begin-mode elementary access *:IntArrays:Rotate*$4!B to the assignment statement *:IntArrays:Rotate*$4, and the terminate-mode elementary access *:IntArrays:Rotate*$3!T follows every terminate-mode elementary access *:IntArrays:Rotate*$4!T produced as a consequence of the iterations.

An elementary access in a given mode to a multiple statement is equivalent to a multiple access expressed in terms of an elementary access for each of the statements which form that multiple statement. The mode of each of these elementary accesses is that of the multiple statement access.

It should be clear that an access to a structured statement is *not* equivalent to an access to each of its component statements. The accesses to these statements will be specified using the multiple statement notation. This point is illustrated by the following example.

Example 3.9

In the execution of the program *IntArrays*, the begin-mode elementary access *:IntArrays:Rotate*$3!B to the **for** statement *:IntArrays:Rotate*$3 is produced at each call to the procedure *Rotate*, by the beginning of the activities involved in the execution of the **for** statement, just once, independently of the number of iterations. The begin-mode elementary access *:IntArrays:Rotate*$3*!B to the multiple statement *:IntArrays:Rotate*$3* is equivalent to the multiple access

   :IntArrays:Rotate$3!B, *:IntArrays:Rotate*$4!B

expressed in terms of a begin-mode elementary access to the **for** statement *:IntArrays:Rotate*$3 and a begin-mode elementary access to the assignment statement *:IntArrays:Rotate*$4 which forms the body of the **for** statement. This multiple statement access is produced not only by the beginning of the activities involved in the execution of the **for** statement, but also, on each iteration, by the beginning of the activities involved in the execution of the assignment statement *:IntArrays:Rotate$4.*

3.2   CONDITIONALS AND EVENTS

A *conditional* is a Boolean expression whose value depends on the state of the target program. The factors of the expression can be program variables, program constants, program enumeration literals, character literals, numeric literals and string literals. A conditional is *true* (*false*) if the expression denoting this conditional is true (false).

Example 3.10

In the program *IntArrays*, the expression

   :IntArrays:Rotate:position = 2

denotes a conditional expressed in terms of the variable *position* declared in the procedure *Rotate*. This conditional assumes the value *true* when the variable assumes the value 2. The expression

   :IntArrays:Rotate:position = *:IntArrays:maxitem*

denotes a conditional which assumes the value *true* when the variable *position* assumes the value of the constant *maxitem* declared in the main program block. The expression

   (*:IntArrays:Rotate:position* = 2) **or** (*:IntArrays:Rotate:position*
   = *:IntArrays:maxitem*)

denotes a conditional which is true on the first and the last iteration of the **for** statement *:IntArrays:Rotate$3.*

An *event* is the specification of an access and a conditional enclosed in square brackets. The symbol '->' separates the access and the conditional, as follows:

   [<access> -> <conditional>]

Let E denote the event $[A \rightarrow C]$ expressed in terms of the access A and the conditional C. The program cycle τ is an *evaluation cycle* of E if the access A is produced at τ. The conditional C is evaluated at τ, and, if true, the event E *occurs* at τ.

As seen in Section 3.1, a write-mode variable access is produced *after* performing a write. It follows that if an event is defined in terms of an access of this type, and this access involves a variable which is included in the specification of the conditional, the modification of the value of the variable, which takes place as a consequence of the access, precedes the evaluation of the conditional.

Example 3.11

In the program *IntArrays*, the event

> $[:IntArrays:Rotate:position!W \rightarrow (:IntArrays:Rotate:position <$
> $2)$ **or** $(:IntArrays:Rotate:position > :IntArrays:maxitem)]$

is defined in terms of a write-mode elementary access to the variable *position* declared in the procedure *Rotate*, and a compound conditional which is true when *position* assumes a value which is not in the value range specified by the type of this variable. The evaluation cycles of this event are the program cycles at which *position* is accessed for write. The conditional is evaluated after accomplishing the write. It follows that this event can be used to detect any write access causing a value-range violation of the value of *position*, if range checks are not inserted by the compiler, for instance.

The notation

> $[<access> \rightarrow]$

stands for an event expressed in terms of a conditional which is always true. This event occurs at each of its evaluation cycles. The notation

> $[\rightarrow <conditional>]$

stands for an event expressed in terms of an access which is produced on every program cycle. This event occurs on each program
cycle such that the conditional is true at that cycle. The notation

[->]

stands for an event which occurs on every program cycle.

Example 3.12

In the program *IntArrays*, the events

[*:IntArrays:Rotate*$1 ->]

and

[*:IntArrays:Rotate*$1!T ->]

occur on a begin-mode and a termination-mode access to the **begin-
end** statement *:IntArrays:Rotate*$1 which forms the body of the
procedure *Rotate*. These events can be used to detect the beginning
and the completion of the execution of the procedure, respectively.

Chapter 4

Registers

Objective

This chapter discusses the management and utilization of the visible portion of the private storage of the program debugging environment. This storage takes the form of *registers*. The scope of the *general registers* is to store partial results of the program debugging experiment. The *special registers* contain information concerning the state of the target program. Examples of special registers are the *block pointers*, which record the names of the blocks being currently executed by the processes which form the target program, and the *statement pointers*, which keep track of the path followed by the control flow of each of these processes.

Contents

In this chapter, we will consider the mechanisms for the management and the utilization of the visible portion of the private storage of PDE, i.e. the PDE *registers*.

As illustrated in Figure 4.1, a register can be a *general register* or a *special register*. The general registers are used to store partial results of the PDE experiment. As will be shown in the next chapter, they can also be used to control the layout of the experiment, for instance, by activating and terminating directives. A general register can be a *user-defined register*, dynamically allocated and deleted by the programmer, or a *predefined register*, allocated and initialized by PDE at the beginning of the PDE session. The predefined registers relieve the programmer of the task of allocating every register required by the current PDE experiment.

The special registers contain information concerning the state of the target program. These registers are allocated and initialized at the beginning of the PDE session. Their values are updated automati-

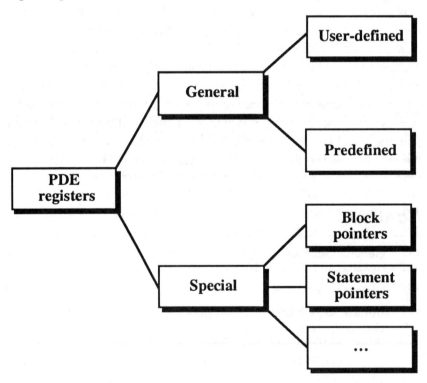

Figure 4.1 Structure of the PDE registers.

cally by PDE during program execution, according to the evolution of the program activity. Examples of special registers are the *block pointers* and the *statement pointers*. The block pointers record the names of the blocks being currently executed by the processes which form the target program. These pointers will allow us to denote the program entities in a new notation, which may represent a useful alternative to the naming rules introduced in Chapter 2. The statement pointers keep track of the program *flow history*, i.e. the path followed by the program control flow. Any implementation of PDE may support additional special registers, aimed at giving special support to the monitoring of those aspects of program behaviour which are of particular interest to the operating environment of that implementation.

4.1 GENERAL REGISTERS

4.1.1 User-defined registers

A user-defined register can be a scalar register or an array register. A scalar register is a recipient for a single value of a scalar type. The scalar types are INTEGER, REAL, BOOLEAN and CHARACTER. An array register consists of a fixed number of elements, which are all of the same scalar type, and are numbered from 1 to the size of the array register. An element of the array register is selected by means of a subscript enclosed in round brackets. The subscript can be an integer or an integer expression. An element of an array register can be used in any construct which uses scalar registers.

User-defined registers can be allocated and deleted by means of the **allocate** and **delete** commands. The **allocate** command has the form

   allocate <register> , ... , <register> : <type specification>

The command parameters include the specification of the identifiers of the registers to be allocated and the type of these registers. For array registers, the type specification includes the array register size, expressed in terms of an integer expression which must be enclosed in round brackets and must produce a positive value. The **allocate** command also initializes the new registers. The initial values are the integer value 0, the real value 0.0, the Boolean value FALSE and the space character. These values apply to both scalar registers and elements of array registers. An **allocate** command can involve an existing register, and in this case it only causes a new initialization of this register. It is an error to use a register before allocating it.

The **delete** command has the form

 delete <register> , ... , <register>

A delete command involving a non-existent register has no effect. It is an error to use a register after deleting it.

Example 4.1

The command

 allocate I1, I2 : INTEGER

allocates the scalar registers I1 and I2 of the type INTEGER and initializes them with value 0. The command

 allocate RR : REAL (20)

allocates the array register RR of 20 elements of the type REAL. RR(1) and RR(20) are the first and the last element. Each element is initialized with value 0.0. The command

 delete I1, RR

deletes the registers I1 and RR.

4.1.2   Predefined registers

The predefined registers are the integer registers A%, B%, ..., Z%, the real registers A%R, B%R, ..., Z%R, the Boolean registers A%B, B%B, ..., Z%B, and the character registers A%C, B%C, ..., Z%C. These registers are allocated and initialized by PDE at the beginning of the PDE session. The initial values are the integer value 0, the real value 0.0, the Boolean value FALSE and the space character. All the operations which can be performed on the user-defined registers can also be performed on the predefined registers. However, the predefined registers cannot be deleted, and their identifiers cannot be used to name user-defined registers.

4.2 BLOCK POINTERS

4.2.1 Sequential programs

If the target program is a sequential program, PDE associates a special register, the *block pointer*, with the program. This special register is denoted by ^. The values it can assume are the path names of the program blocks (denoted as specified in Section 2.2) and the *undefined* block path name ^?. At any given program cycle, the value of the block pointer is equal to the path name of the *current block*, i.e. the block containing the statement being executed at that cycle (the *current statement*).

The block pointer is updated by PDE automatically, in accordance with the activity of the target program, as stated by the following rules:

- the initial value of the block pointer is the undefined block path name ^?;

- on beginning of execution of a given program statement, the block pointer is accessed, and its current value is replaced with the path name of the block containing this statement;

- on termination of program execution, the value of the block pointer is equal to the path name of the block containing the last statement executed.

Example 4.2

Let us refer again to the Pascal program *IntArrays* introduced in Chapter 3 (see Figure 3.1). In this program, the values which can be assumed by the block pointer ^ are the path name *:IntArrays* of the main program block, the path name *:IntArrays:Rotate* of the procedure *Rotate* and the undefined block path name ^?. The initial value of ^ is ^?. On execution of the first program statement, i.e. the statement *:IntArrays*$1, this value is replaced with the path name *:IntArrays* of the main program block. When the control flow enters the procedure *Rotate*, the current value of ^ is replaced with the path name *:IntArrays:Rotate*.

4.2.2   Concurrent programs

Various programming language constructs have been proposed for writing concurrent programs [Andrews, 1983], [Ben-Ari, 1990], [Krishnamurthy, 1989]. Concurrent execution can be specified at the statement level, for instance, by means of the concurrent statement **cobegin-coend**, which has the form

> **cobegin**
>   <statement>;
>   <statement>;
>   ...;
>   <statement>
> **coend**

This statement activates a process for each one of its component statements. PDE identifies a process specified at the statement level by the name of the statement and the symbol 'l', as follows:

> <statement name>l

The statement name will be denoted by using the statement naming rules illustrated in Section 2.6.

Example 4.3

The program *ConcStmt* shown in Figure 4.2 specifies concurrent execution of three processes by means of a concurrent statement **cobegin-coend**. PDE identifies these processes by using the statement naming rules. Thus, these processes will be denoted by *:ConcStmt*$3l, *:ConcStmt*$5l and *:ConcStmt*$7l, respectively.

```
      {:ConcStmt}  program ConcStmt (...);
                       ...
   {:ConcStmt$1}  begin {ConcStmt}
         {$2}        cobegin
         {$3}           repeat {first process}
         {$4}              ...
                       until false;
         {$5}           repeat {second process}
         {$6}              ...
                       until false;
         {$7}           repeat {third process}
         {$8}              ...
                       until false;
                    coend
                 end. {ConcStmt}
```

Figure 4.2 Program *ConcStmt* written in a concurrent language specifying concurrent execution by means of the **cobegin-coend** statement.

Concurrent execution can be also specified at the block level, for example by *process declarations*. A possible notation for these declarations consists of a heading and a body. The heading gives the process identifier, the body has the same structure as a Pascal subprogram body, i.e. a declaration part and a statement part, as follows:

process <process identifier>;
   ... {declaration part}
begin
   ... {statement part}
end

PDE identifies a process specified by a process declaration by the path name of the block introduced by the declaration and the symbol 'l', as follows:

   <block path name>l

The block path name will be denoted by using the block naming rules presented in Section 2.2.

Example 4.4

The program *Occasions* shown in Figure 4.3 is written in a concurrent language using shared variables and semaphores for process cooperation and synchronization. In this language, concurrent execution is indicated by means of process declarations. The program monitors the occurrence of occasions of different classes. The classes are numbered from 1 to the value of the program constant *maxoclass*. The program consists of two processes, *Observer* and *Reporter*. *Observer* is responsible for detecting the occurrence of occasions and counting the number of them for each class. *Reporter* periodically displays the distribution of the occasions in the different classes. The display period is stated by the value of the constant *maxocount* in terms of the number of occasions to be detected before performing a display.

Observer and *Reporter* share access to the array *partial*, the *i*th element of which contains the number of occasions of the class *i* detected since the previous display. The procedure *Clear* is used by *Observer* to clear the contents of *partial*, and by *Reporter* to clear the contents of the local array *total*, which stores the total number of occasions of each class.

Two semaphores, *osem* and *rsem*, synchronize the activities of the two processes and ensure mutual exclusion in the accesses to the array *partial*. The declarations of the semaphores include assignment statements aimed at initializing them with value 0.

PDE identifies the processes *Observer* and *Reporter* by using the block naming rules. Thus, *Observer* is denoted by :*Occasions*:*Observer*|, and *Reporter* is denoted by :*Occasions*:*Reporter*|.

In a concurrent program, we have several flows of control, one flow for each process. PDE associates a block pointer with each process. The block pointer of a given process is denoted by the name of the process and the symbol '^', as follows:

<process name>^

Let *P1*|, *P2*|, ..., *Pn*| be the process names. The values which

```
        {:Occasions}        program Occasions;
  {:Occasions:maxoclass}        const maxoclass = ...;
  {:Occasions:maxocount}           maxocount = ...;
  {:Occasions:nonegint}        type nonegint = 0..maxint;
    {:Occasions:oclass}           oclass = 1..maxoclass;
  {:Occasions:occarray}           occarray = array [oclass]
                                     of nonegint;
    {:Occasions:partial}        var partial : occarray;
     {:Occasions:osem}           osem,
     {:Occasions:rsem}           rsem : semaphore := 0;
    {:Occasions:Clear}        procedure Clear (
 {:Occasions:Clear.occarr}        var occarr : occarray);
{:Occasions:Clear:position}       var position : oclass;
   {:Occasions:Clear$1}        begin {Clear}
                 {$2}            for position := 1 to maxoclass
                 {$3}            do occarr [position] := 0
                                end; {Clear}


  {:Occasions:Observer}        process Observer;
{:Occasions:Observer.class}       var class : oclass;
{:Occasions:Observer.count}          count : 0..maxocount;
{:Occasions:Observer.Detect}      procedure Detect (
{:Occasions:Observer:Detect:class}    var class : oclass);
{:Occasions:Observer:Detect$1}    begin {Detect}
              {$...}              ...    {detect the occurrence of an
                                            occasion}
                                end; {Detect}
{:Occasions:Observer$1}        begin {Observer}
                 {$2}            repeat
                 {$3}             Clear (partial);
                 {$4}             count := 0;
                 {$5}             while count < maxocount
                 {$6}             do   begin
                 {$7}                  Detect (class);
                 {$8}                  partial [class] :=
                                          partial [class] + 1;
                 {$9}                  count := count + 1
                                      end;
                {$10}            V (rsem);
                {$11}            P (osem)
                                until false
                                end; {Observer}
```

Figure 4.3 Program *Occasions* written in a concurrent language specifying concurrent execution by means of process declarations.

```
        {:Occasions:Reporter}          process Reporter;
     {:Occasions:Reporter:total}         var total : occarray;
   {:Occasions:Reporter:Display}         procedure Display (
{:Occasions:Reporter:Display:occarr}        var occarr : occarray);
  {:Occasions:Reporter:Display$1}         begin {Display}
                {$...}                      ...   {display the contents
                                                    of array occarr}
                                         end; {Display}
   {:Occasions:Reporter:Addocc}          procedure Addocc (
  {:Occasions:Reporter:Addocc:t}            var t,
  {:Occasions:Reporter:Addocc:p}            p : occarray);
{:Occasions:Reporter:Addocc:position}     var position : oclass;
 {:Occasions:Reporter:Addocc$1}          begin {Addocc}
                {$2}                        for position := 1 to maxoclass
                {$3}                        do t [position] :=
                                                t [position] + p [position]
                                         end; {Addocc}
   {:Occasions:Reporter$1}               begin {Reporter}
                {$2}                        Clear (total);
                {$3}                        repeat
                {$4}                          P (rsem);
                {$5}                          Addocc (total, partial);
                {$6}                          V (osem);
                {$7}                          Display (total)
                                            until false
                                         end {Reporter}

                                         end. {Occasions}
```

Figure 4.3 *Continued.*

can be assumed by the block pointer $Pil^\wedge$ of the process Pil are the path names of the blocks whose statements can be executed by Pil and the undefined block path name $^\wedge?$. At any given program cycle, the value of $Pil^\wedge$ is equal to the path name of the current block of the process Pil, i.e. the program block containing the statement being executed by Pil at that cycle (the current statement of Pil).

$Pil^\wedge$ is updated by PDE automatically, as stated by the following rules:

• the initial value of $Pil^\wedge$ is the undefined block path name $^\wedge?$;

- on beginning of execution of a given statement as a consequence of the activity of the process *Pil*, *Pil*^ is accessed, and its current value is replaced with the path name of the block containing this statement;

- on termination of *Pil*, the value of *Pil*^ is equal to the path name of the block containing the last statement executed by *Pil*.

Example 4.5
_____

In the program *Occasions*, two block pointers will be maintained by PDE, one for the process *Observer*, which will be denoted by *:Occasions:Observer|*^, and one for the process *Reporter*, which will be denoted by *:Occasions:Reporter|*^. Let us refer to *:Occasions:Observer|*^. The values this pointer can assume are the path name *:Occasions:Observer* of the block of the process and the path names *:Occasions:Clear* and *:Occasions:Observer:Detect* of the procedures *Clear* and *Detect* which can be executed by *Observer*. The initial value of *:Occasions:Observer|*^ is the undefined block path name ^?. PDE updates the pointer automatically as a consequence of the activity of the process *Observer*. For instance, on starting up execution of the procedure *Clear*, the current value of *:Occasions:Observer|*^ is replaced with the path name *:Occasions:Clear*.

_____

4.2.3   Relative block path names

In Section 2.1 we saw that the scope rules of the programming language, based on the *dynamic* program activity, are inadequate at the PDE level, and we have demonstrated that a *static* notation is needed to identify the blocks of the target program according to the program structure. An *absolute* notation of this type was introduced in Section 2.2. In this notation, a given block is denoted with reference to the program tree representation, by means of an absolute path name expressed in terms of the sequence of the identifiers of the blocks in the path from the root of the tree to this block.

In Section 2.8, we pointed out a drawback of the absolute path name notation, i.e. the need to type a long path name to identify á deeply nested block. We will now introduce another static notation for denoting the program blocks. This *relative* notation is based on the notion of the current block. In certain situations, this notation can be a useful alternative to the absolute notation. With respect to alias definition, the new notation has the advantage of relieving the programmer from the task of issuing the **alias** command, which may be both distracting and error-prone, especially if the list of the active aliases has grown to such extent that it is difficult to remember them all.

In the relative block path name notation, a block is denoted with reference to the program tree representation, by means of a block pointer followed by the identifiers of the blocks in the tree path from the block identified by the block pointer to that block. In the path name, the symbol ':' separates the block identifiers, as follows:

<block pointer><block identifier>:<block identifier>: ...
  :<block identifier>

Thus, in a sequential program, the current block is simply denoted by ^, and the block path name

^<block identifier>:<block identifier>: ... :<block identifier>

is a relative block path name corresponding to a path starting from the current block.

In a sequential program, the block pointer can be omitted from relative block path names. In this case, a relative block path name can be distinguished from an absolute path name by the absence of the initial symbol ':'. It should be noted that, in this abbreviated form, an entity of a sequential program declared in the current block is simply denoted by the entity identifier.

Example 4.6

Let us refer again to the program *IntArrays* introduced in Chapter 3 (see Figure 3.1). Suppose that, in an interactive PDE session, we have placed a breakpoint at a statement of the procedure *Rotate*. On reaching this breakpoint, by using the relative block path name notation, we can denote the first and the last statement of this procedure by ^$1 and ^$$ (which can be abbreviated in $1 and $$), and the variable *position* declared in *Rotate* by *^position* (which can be abbreviated in *position*).

A *pointer modifier* can be interposed between the block pointer and the block identifiers, as follows:

<block pointer><pointer modifier><block identifier>:<block identifier>: ... :<block identifier>

The pointer modifier moves the starting block of the tree path to an ancestor of the current block. For instance, if the block *E* specified by the block pointer is not the main program block, modifier '^' denotes a path starting from the block *E'* enclosing the block *E*; if *E'* is not the main program block, modifier '^^' denotes a path starting from the block *E"* enclosing the block *E'*; and so on. Thus, in a sequential program, the block enclosing the current block is denoted by ^^, and the block path name

^^<block identifier>:<block identifier>: ... :<block identifier>

is a relative block path name corresponding to a path starting from the block enclosing the current block.

Example 4.7

In the program *IntArrays*, on reaching a breakpoint in the procedure *Rotate*, the first statement of the main program block can be denoted by ^^$1, and the constant *maxitem* declared in this block can be denoted by ^^*maxitem*.

4.3   STATEMENT POINTERS

4.3.1   Sequential programs

PDE associates a special register, the *statement pointer*, with each block of a sequential program. The statement pointer of a given block is denoted by the path name of this block and the symbol '@', as follows:

<block path name>@

The values which can be assumed by the statement pointer $B@$ of a block whose path name is B are the names of the statements of that block (denoted as in Section 2.6), and the special statement name $@?$, called the *undefined* statement name.

$B@$ is updated by PDE automatically, according to the activity of the target program, as stated by the following rules:

- the initial value of $B@$ is the undefined statement name $@?$;
- on beginning of execution of a statement of the block B, $B@$ is accessed, and its current value is replaced with the name of this statement;
- after abandoning the block B, the value of $B@$ is equal to the name of the last statement executed in that block.

Example 4.8

In the program *IntArrays* shown in Figure 3.1, the statement pointer of the procedure *Rotate* is denoted by *:IntArrays:Rotate@*. The values which can be assumed by this pointer are the names *:IntArrays:Rotate$1*, *:IntArrays:Rotate$2*, ..., *:IntArrays:Rotate$5* of the procedure statements and the undefined statement name $@?$.

4.3.2   Concurrent programs

In a concurrent program, if a block is shared by two or more processes, PDE associates a statement pointer with this block for each of these processes. This pointer is denoted by the name of the process and the path name of the block, followed by the symbol '@', as follows:

<process name><block path name>@

Let $P1|$, $P2|$, ... , $Pn|$ be the names of the processes which share access to a block whose path name is SB. The values which can be assumed by the statement pointer $Pi|SB@$ of the process $Pi|$ are the names of the statements of SB and the undefined statement name $@?$.

Pi|SB@ is updated by PDE automatically, as stated by the following rules:

- the initial value of *Pi|SB@* is the undefined statement name @?;
- on beginning of execution of a statement of the block *SB* as a consequence of the activity of the process *Pi|*, *Pi|SB@* is accessed, and its current value is replaced with the name of this statement;
- after *Pi|* has abandoned the block *SB*, the value of *Pi|SB@* is equal to the name of the last statement executed in *SB* by *Pi|*.

Example 4.9

In the program *Occasions* shown in Figure 4.3, the procedure *Clear* is shared between the processes *Observer* and *Reporter*. This subprogram is therefore involved in two different control flows. PDE associates two statement pointers with *Clear*, one for *Observer,* which is denoted by *:Occasions:Observer|:Occasions:Clear@*, and one for *Reporter*, which is denoted by *:Occasions:Reporter|:Occasions:Clear@*. The values which can be assumed by these pointers are the names *:Occasions:Clear*$1, *:Occasions:Clear*$2 and *:Occasions:Clear*$3 of the statements of *Clear*, and the undefined statement name @?.

Finally, if a block of a concurrent program is local to a given process, and can therefore be involved in a single control flow, PDE treats this block in the same way as a block of a sequential program.

Example 4.10

In the program *Occasions*, the procedure *Display* is local to the process *Reporter*. Therefore, PDE associates a single statement pointer with *Display*. This pointer is denoted by *:Occasions:Reporter:Display@*. The values it can assume are the names *:Occasions:Reporter:Display*$1, *:Occasions:Reporter:Display*$2, ... of the statements of *Display*, and the undefined statement name @?.

4.3.3   Recursive subprograms

As seen in Section 2.2, in the execution of a recursive subprogram, a new activation of the subprogram block is generated at each recursive subprogram call. PDE associates a statement pointer with each one of these activations.

Example 4.11

Let us refer to the function *Fact* of the program *Factorials* (see Figure 2.9). PDE associates a statement pointer with each activation of *Fact*. By using the notation for specifying recursive subprogram activations, which has been introduced in Section 2.2, the pointers for the first, the second and the most recent activation will be denoted by *:Factorials:Fact~1@*, *:Factorials:Fact~2@* and *:Factorials:Fact~~@*, respectively. By using the abbreviated notation to specify the most recent activation, the pointer for this activation can be also denoted simply by *:Factorials:Fact@*.

4.3.4   Current statement pointers

An interesting application of the relative block path name notation and the statement pointers is to identify the current statement of a sequential program by ^@, i.e. the statement being executed in the current block. By using the abbreviated notation for relative block path names, quantity ^@ can also be denoted simply by @. This quantity will be called the *current statement pointer* of the sequential program. It should be clear, however, that this pointer is *not* a new special register, but only the result of a combination of quantities contained in other special registers (the block pointer, and the statement pointer of the current block).

Let us now consider a concurrent program, and let *P1|*, *P2|*, ..., *Pn|* be the names of the active processes. The current statement of the process *Pi|* is identified by a combination of the quantities contained in the block pointer of the process *Pi|* and the statement pointer of the current block. The resulting quantity will be called the current statement pointer of *Pi|*, and will be denoted by *Pi|@*.

Example 4.12

In the program *Occasions*, the current statement pointers of the processes *Observer* and *Reporter* are denoted by *:Occasions:Observer*|@ and *:Occasions:Reporter*|@, respectively.

Table 4.1 summarizes the names of the block pointers and the statement pointers for both sequential and concurrent programs.

Table 4.1 – Block and statement pointers.

^	Block pointer of a sequential program.
Pi|^	Block pointer of the process *Pi*| of a concurrent program.
B@	Statement pointer of the block *B* of a sequential program.
Pi|*SB*@	Statement pointer of the shared block *SB* and the process *Pi*| of a concurrent program.
LB@	Statement pointer of the local block *LB* of a concurrent program.
@	Current statement pointer of a sequential program.
Pi|@	Current statement pointer of the process *Pi*| of a concurrent program.

4.4 OTHER SPECIAL REGISTERS

In addition to the block pointers and the statement pointers, any implementation of PDE may support other special registers, which can contain further information concerning the state of the target program. An example is the *static lexical level register _SLL*. At any given program cycle, this register records the static lexical level of the block containing the declaration of the program entity involved in the program operation performed at that cycle. Examples of applications of this special register will be shown in Chapter 9.

4.5   USING REGISTERS

4.5.1   Assigning a value to a register

A new value can be assigned to a scalar register or an element of an array register by using the assignment command, which has the form

<register> := <PDE scalar expression>

Execution of this command evaluates the PDE scalar expression and assigns the result to the named register. The register and the value of the expression must be of the same type. The factors of a PDE scalar expression can be scalar registers, elements of array registers, numeric literals, Boolean literals and characters.

4.5.2   Input and output

Input and output operations involving the values of the registers can be performed by means of the **rget** and the **rput** commands. The **rget** command has the form

rget <register> , ... , <register> **from** <file>

The registers can be scalar registers or elements of array registers. For each register, this command reads a sequence of characters from the specified file, converts this sequence into a value of the same type as this register, and assigns this value to the register. The file specification can be omitted. In this case, the keyword **from** must also be omitted, and the character sequences are received from the console.

The **rput** command has the form

rput <rput parameter> , ... , <rput parameter> **to** <file>

An rput parameter can be a PDE scalar expression, a special register or a string literal. This command interprets the value of each parameter according to its type, and converts this value into a sequence of characters. The contents of the specified file are replaced with these sequences. If the file does not exist, it is created. The file specification can be omitted. In this case, the keyword **to** must also be omitted, and the character sequences are transmitted to the console.

Output can be appended to a file by issuing an **rput** command with the **append** attribute, as follows

>   **rput** <rput parameter> , ... , <rput parameter> **append to**
>   <file>

A permanent redirection from/to a given file of the data input and output generated by the **rget** and the **rput** commands can be obtained by means of the **permanent input** and the **permanent output** commands, introduced in Section 2.7.

4.5.3   Altering the program control flow

The assignment command can be used to alter the control flow of the target program. For instance, if we replace the value of the block pointer of a sequential program with the path name of a given subprogram, we cause execution to continue in this subprogram, at the statement specified by the statement pointer of this subprogram.

Example 4.13

In the program *IntArrays*, suppose we have placed a breakpoint at a statement of the procedure *Rotate*. On reaching this breakpoint, we can force execution to resume at the subprogram call in the main program block by issuing the assignment command

> $^\wedge := :IntArrays$

We can also cause execution to continue at a specific statement of a given block by assigning the name of this statement to the current statement pointer. This is equivalent to a modification of the contents of both the block pointer and the statement pointer of the block.

Example 4.14

In the program *IntArrays*, on reaching a breakpoint, we can cause execution to continue at the first statement of the main program block by issuing the assignment command

@ := :*IntArrays*$1

This command is equivalent to the command pair

:IntArrays@ := `:*IntArrays*$1
^ := :*IntArrays*

The implementation of PDE may restrict this usage of the assignment statement, by limiting the possible assignments to the statements of the current block, for instance.

Of course, the techniques analysed so far can also be used to alter the control flows of the processes of a concurrent program.

4.5.4   Assigning a value to a program variable

In Section 2.7, we described the **set** command, which can be used to replace the value of a program variable with that of an expression defined in terms of the program entities. We will now introduce a new command, the **rset** command, which makes it possible to replace the value of a variable with that of an expression defined in terms of the registers. This command is as follows:

rset <variable name> **to** <PDE scalar expression>

The execution of this command evaluates the PDE scalar expression and assigns the result to the named variable. This variable and the value of the expression must be of structurally compatible types.

The implementation may restrict the applicability of the **rset** command. Under this respect, the considerations made in Section 2.7 for the **set** command apply to the **rset** command as well.

Chapter 5

Commands and directives

Objective

This chapter presents the mechanisms for the definition of the layout of the program debugging experiment. The layout is expressed in terms of the dynamic activation and termination of *directives*. A directive is the specification of a *command* to be executed conditionally. The command denotes manipulation of one or more registers or program entities. The condition is defined in terms of an *event* and a *guard* expressed as a function of the values of the registers.

Contents

5.1   COMMANDS

A *command* is the specification of an action to be performed by PDE. This action is expressed in terms of manipulation of one or more registers and/or program entities. Commands can be simple or structured. A *simple* command expresses an elementary PDE action. A *structured* command expresses a composite action in terms of other simple or structured commands. A simple command must be written in a single line; the symbol '\' on the right side of a line can be used to carry a long simple command over into the next line.

Several simple commands have been presented in the previous chapters. We will now describe the structured commands which make it possible to specify command composition, selection and repetition.

5.1.1   Compounding commands

Two or more commands can be grouped to form a single command by means of the compound command. This structured command takes the form of a sequence of simple and/or structured commands enclosed in curly brackets, as follows:

```
{
  <command>
  <command>
     ...
  <command>
}
```

The component commands will be executed in succession. A compound command can be used in any construct which uses a single command. Two or more component commands can be written on the same line, and, in this case, they will be separated by the symbol ';'.

5.1.2   Selection

The selection command is used to choose from a number of alternatives. This structured command takes the form of a sequence of switch elements bracketed by the delimiters **switch** and **end switch**, as follows:

```
switch
  <switch element>
  <switch element>
     ...
```

```
    <switch element>
  end  switch
```

A switch element consists of the keyword **case** followed by a condition and a command sequence. The condition is a PDE scalar expression whose evaluation produces a Boolean value. The symbol ':' separates the condition and the commands, as follows:

```
  case <condition> :
    <command>
    <command>
       ...
    <command>
```

The selection command evaluates the conditions in the switch elements in succession, and executes the commands in the first switch element whose condition is true. If no condition is true, the selection command has no other effect.

Example 5.1

Here we give an example of a selection command which implements an **if-then** scheme:

```
  switch
    case U% > V% :
      X% := U%
      U% := V%
      V% := X%
  end  switch
```

This command exchanges the values of the predefined registers U% and V% if the value of U% is greater than that of V%. The command includes a single switch element, whose condition is expressed in terms of U% and V%. The predefined register X% is used as a temporary recipient for the initial value of U%.

The following selection command implements an **if-then-else** scheme:

```
  switch
    case I% > J% :
      U% := I% + J%; V% := I% - J%
```

```
    case TRUE :
       U% := I% - J%; V% := I% + J%
  end  switch
```

In this example, the assignment commands in the second switch element are executed only if the value of the predefined register I% is less than or equal to the value of the predefined register J%.

5.1.3   Repetition

Iterated command execution can be specified by means of the repetition command. This structured command has the form of a command sequence bracketed by the delimiters **loop** and **end loop**, as follows:

```
loop
   <command>
   <command>
      ...
   <command>
end  loop
```

The execution is complete when the loop is abandoned as a consequence of the execution of the simple command **exit**. This command has the form

```
   exit <condition>
```

It completes the execution of the smallest enclosing loop if the condition is true. The condition can be omitted. An **exit** command with no condition specification is equivalent to an **exit** command specifying a condition which is always true.

Example 5.2

The repetitive command which follows implements a **while** iteration scheme:

```
loop
   exit <condition>
```

   ...
   end loop

In this application, the condition controlling the completion of the iterations is a parameter of an **exit** command.

The repetitive command which follows implements a **repeat-until** iteration scheme:

   loop

      ...
      exit <condition>
   end loop

Finally, let COUNTER, INITIAL, INCREMENT and FINAL be user-defined registers of the type INTEGER. The repetitive command which follows implements a **for** iteration scheme:

COUNTER := INITIAL
loop
   exit COUNTER > FINAL

   ...
   COUNTER := COUNTER + INCREMENT
end loop

COUNTER is used to control the iterations, INITIAL and FINAL specify the initial and final values of COUNTER, and INCREMENT specifies the value to be added to COUNTER at each iteration.

5.1.4 Command scripts

A command sequence can be associated with an identifier by means of the *command script* (or *c-script*, for short) PDE construct. In a c-script, the identifier is preceded by the keyword **script** and followed by the command sequence enclosed in curly brackets, as follows:

script <c-script identifier> {
   <command>
   <command>

     ...

```
    <command>
  }
```

A c-script can be executed by means of the simple command **exec**, which is as follows:

  exec <c-script identifier>

The execution of a c-script consists of the execution of its component commands in succession.

The c-script construct implements the classic programming language concept of a subprogram at the PDE command level. Data communication to/from c-scripts takes place via the global environment of the registers.

Example 5.3

The c-script NEW_ELEMENTS which follows creates an array register called ELEMENTS:

```
  script NEW_ELEMENTS {
    allocate MAX : INTEGER
    rget MAX
    allocate ELEMENTS : INTEGER (MAX)
  }
```

In this c-script, the first command allocates the user-defined register MAX of the type INTEGER, the second command reads the number of the array elements from the console and stores this number into MAX, the third command allocates the array register. This script can be executed by issuing the command

  exec NEW_ELEMENTS

The c-script DISPLAY_ELEMENTS which follows displays the value of the elements of the array register ELEMENTS at the console:

```
  script DISPLAY_ELEMENTS {
    allocate CURRENT : INTEGER
    CURRENT := 1
    loop
      rput ELEMENTS (CURRENT)
```

```
        CURRENT := CURRENT + 1
        exit CURRENT > MAX
     end  loop
     delete CURRENT
   }
```

The elements are processed by a repetitive command. The user-defined register CURRENT is used to select the element to be processed by the current iteration. This script can be executed by issuing the command

exec DISPLAY_ELEMENTS

5.2   DIRECTIVES

A *directive* is the specification of a command to be conditionally executed on the occurrence of a given event. Directives can be simple or guarded. A *simple directive* is the specification of an event and a command, as follows:

<event> <command>

A directive always specifies a single command; two or more commands can be included in a directive by grouping them into a compound command.

Example 5.4

Let us refer again to the program *IntArrays* introduced in Chapter 3 (see Figure 3.1), and let *Rt* be an alias for the path name *:IntArrays:Rotate* of the procedure *Rotate*, as is defined by the command

alias Rt := *:IntArrays:Rotate*

(we will use this alias definition in several other examples in this chapter). The simple directive which follows detects the beginning of the execution of *Rotate*:

[Rt1 ->] **rput** 'Executing Rotate...'

In this directive, the event is defined in terms of a begin-mode elementary access to the first statement of *Rotate*, and of a conditional which is always true. The command is an **rput** simple command causing the display of a warning message at the console.

On each call to *Rotate*, the simple directive which follows displays the position occupied after the rotation by each element of the array *circular* whose value is equal to 0:

[*Rt:circular*!W -> *Rt:circular* [*Rt:position*] = 0] **put** *Rt:position*

In this directive, the event is defined in terms of a write-mode elementary access to *circular*, and of a conditional which is true when the value of the element of *circular* selected by the variable *position* controlling the iterations is equal to 0. The command is a **put** command which displays the value of *position* at the console.

A *guarded directive* is the specification of a guard, an event and a command, as follows:

<guard> <event> <command>

The *guard* is a PDE Boolean expression.

An *active* directive is a directive processed concurrently with the execution of the target program, according to the values assumed by the program entities and by the registers included in the directive specification. An active directive can *terminate*. After termination, the directive produces no more effects. PDE has no memory of the terminated directives.

Later in this section we will introduce the commands for activating and terminating directives dynamically. On activation of a directive, PDE generates a *directive number* (or *d-number*, for short) and associates this number with that directive. The d-numbers are aimed at univocally identifying the directives. They are generated according to the following rule:

If the directive D_j is activated after the directive D_i, then the d-number of D_j is greater than that of D_i.

An active directive is *open* if it is either a simple directive or a guarded directive whose guard is true. On each program cycle, the active directives are considered in the order of activation (i.e. in the order of increasing d-numbers). For each directive which is open, if the event specified by this directive occurs at that cycle, then the corresponding command is executed. If no directive is open, or no event occurs, the cycle has no other effect.

The command in a given directive may modify the value of the guards of that and of the other directives, thus dynamically altering the set of open directives.

Example 5.5

In the program *IntArrays*, on each access made by the procedure *Rotate* to the constant *:IntArrays:maxitem* declared in the main program block, the directives which follow indicate the statement causing the access (the directive activation numbers are shown on the left side of each directive, enclosed in round brackets):

$$[\ Rt\$1 ->] \ G\%B := \text{TRUE} \hspace{3cm} (1)$$
$$G\%B \quad [\ :IntArrays:maxitem ->] \ \textbf{rput} \ @ \hspace{1.3cm} (2)$$
$$[\ Rt\$1!T ->] \ G\%B := \text{FALSE} \hspace{2.3cm} (3)$$

(1) and (3) are simple directives, (2) is a guarded directive. The guard is expressed in terms of the Boolean predefined register G%B. As seen in Section 4.1, the initial value of a register of this type is FALSE. It follows that this directive is initially closed. On the beginning of the execution of *Rotate*, the assignment command in the first directive sets G%B to TRUE, so opening the directive (2). On each access to *maxitem*, the command in the directive (2) displays the value of the current statement pointer of *IntArrays* at the console. Finally, on termination of the execution of *Rotate*, the assignment command in the directive (3) sets G%B to FALSE, thereby closing the directive (2). In this way, no display will be generated by an access to *maxitem* produced when the control flow is not in *Rotate*.

5.2.1   Activating and terminating directives

Directives can be activated and terminated by means of the **activate** and the **terminate** simple commands. The **activate** command has the form

activate <directive>

The keyword **activate** is optional, and can be omitted. This command generates a d-number, associates this d-number with the specified directive, displays the d-number at the console, and finally activates the directive.

Example 5.6

In the program *IntArrays*, the command

activate [*Rt:circular*!W ->] C% := C% + 1

generates a d-number and displays it at the console. It then activates a directive which counts the write accesses made by the procedure *Rotate* to the array *circular* by incrementing the value of the predefined register C% on each of these accesses. In the abbreviated form, this command can be written as follows:

[*Rt:circular*!W ->] C% := C% + 1

From now on, we will always omit the keyword **activate**.

The **terminate** command has the form

terminate <d-number list>

This command terminates the directives whose d-numbers are included in the specified list of d-numbers. The d-numbers which do not correspond to active directives are ignored. A d-number list consists of one or more d-numbers separated by the symbol ',' as follows:

<d-number>, <d-number>, …, <d-number>

In this list, the d-number of the directive activated most recently can be denoted by '~', and the d-numbers in a given range can be denoted by the lower bound and the upper bound of the range separated by the symbol '..', as follows:

<lower d-number>..<upper d-number>

Example 5.7

The command

terminate 1..5, 10, ~

terminates the directives whose d-numbers are in the range 1 to 5, the directive whose d-number is 10, and the most recently activated directive. The d-numbers which do not correspond to active directives are ignored.

The command

terminate 1..~

terminates all active directives.

A directive cannot activate or terminate other directives. It follows that the **activate** and the **terminate** commands cannot be included in the command part of a directive, but must be issued from the console.

5.2.2   Directive scripts

The command script construct, introduced in the previous section, allows us to associate a sequence of directives with an identifier by defining a command script consisting of an **activate** command for each directive in the sequence. These directives will be activated by executing the script by means of the **exec** simple command. They will be terminated by issuing a **terminate** command specifying the range of the d-numbers associated with the directives on the execution of the script.

We will use the term *directive script* (or *d-script*, for short) to identify a command script including one or more **activate** commands. As stated previously, a directive cannot activate or terminate other directives. It follows that an **exec** command executing a d-script cannot be included in the command part of a directive, but must be issued from the console.

Example 5.8

In the program *IntArrays*, at each call to the procedure *Rotate*, the directives in the d-script EQZ which follows count the elements of the array *circular* whose value is equal to 0:

```
script EQZ {
  [ Rt$1 -> ] allocate COUNT : INTEGER                    (1)
  [ Rt$4 -> Rt:circular [Rt:position] = 0 ] \             (2)
    COUNT := COUNT+ 1
  [ Rt$1!T -> ] {                                         (3)
    rput COUNT
    delete COUNT
    }
}
```

In this script, on the beginning of the execution of *Rotate*, the directive (1) allocates the user-defined register COUNT and initializes it to 0. The directive (2) monitors the execution of the statement *:IntArrays:Rotate*$4 which forms the body of the **for** statement in *Rotate*. This directive increments COUNT if the value of the array element being processed by the current iteration is equal to 0. On termination of the execution of *Rotate*, the directive (3) displays the result at the console and deletes COUNT. The directives in this script can be activated by issuing the command

exec EQZ

D-scripts are especially useful in a complex PDE experiment involving subsequent activations and terminations of the same directive or group of directives. As seen previously, PDE has no memory of the terminated directives. It follows that, if one or more terminated directives must be re-activated, the programmer has to issue new **activate** commands and rewrite the directives. By including these directives in a d-script, their re-activation can be obtained simply by issuing an **exec** command for this d-script.

5.2.3 Displaying the active directives

The active directives can be displayed by means of the **directive display** simple command, which has the form

directive display <d-number list> **to** <file>

For each active directive whose d-number is included in the specified d-number list, this command produces a display of that directive in the form of a sequence of characters. The contents of the specified file are replaced by these sequences. If the file does not exist, it is created. The file specification can be omitted. In this case, the keyword **to** must also be omitted, and the character sequences are transmitted to the console. D-numbers in the d-number list which do not correspond to active directives are ignored.

A directive display can be appended to a file by issuing a **directive display** command with the **append** attribute, as follows:

directive display <d-number list> **append to** <file>

A permanent redirection to a given file of the data output generated by the **directive display** command can be obtained by means of the **permanent output** command, described in Section 2.7.

Example 5.9

The command

directive display 1..10, ~ **append to** OUTFILE

produces a display of the directives whose d-numbers are in the range 1 to 10, and of the most recently activated directive. The d-numbers which do not correspond to active directives are ignored. The display is appended to the file OUTFILE.

The command

directive display 1..~

displays all the active directives. The display is produced at the console.

5.3   PROCESS STATES

5.3.1   Sequential programs

The execution of a sequential program generates a single process. At any given time, this process can be either in *run* state or in *break* state (Figure 5.1). In run state, the process carries on the elaborations specified by the program, in break state these elaborations are suspended. The run state is the initial process state.

The **break** simple command switches the process from run state into break state. This command has the form

break

If the process is in break state, the command has no effect.

The **run** simple command switches the process from break state into run state. This command has the form

run

It resumes the process elaborations in the block specified by the block pointer, at the statement specified by the statement pointer of this block. If the process is in run state, this command has no effect.

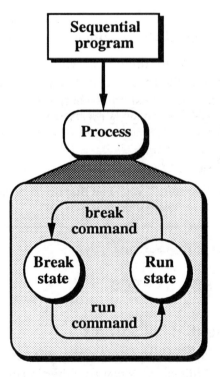

Figure 5.1 The states of the process generated by the execution of a sequential program.

A break trap is the effect of the execution of a **break** command. As seen in Section 1.1, a break trap can be asynchronous or synchronous. An asynchronous break trap is produced by the programmer who issues a **break** command from the console. A synchronous break trap is produced by a directive including a **break** command. A breakpoint is produced by a directive specifying an event defined in terms of an access to a program statement.

When a process enters the break state, the programmer can inspect the effects of the process activity by means of the **put** and **rput** commands. He will use the **put** command to display the value of the program defined entities, and the **rput** command to display the value of the registers. In particular, from an inspection of the value of the current statement pointer, the programmer will identify the point reached by the process control flow. This will be especially useful after an asynchronous break trap.

Example 5.10

In the program *IntArrays*, a breakpoint is placed at the beginning of the execution of *Rotate* as follows:

> [*Rt*$1 ->] **break**

In this directive, the event is defined in terms of a begin-mode elementary access to the first statement of *Rotate*. On the occurrence of this event, a **break** command is issued causing the process generated by the execution of *IntArrays* to enter break state.

The simple directive which follows generates a synchronous break trap on the first and on the last iteration of the **for** statement in *Rotate*:

> [*Rt*$4 -> (*Rt:position* = :*IntArrays:maxitem*) \
>   **or** (*Rt:position* = 2)] {
> **break**
> **put** 'position: ', *Rt:position*
> }

In this directive, the event is defined in terms of a begin-mode elementary access to the statement *Rt*$4 which forms the body of the **for** statement, and of a conditional which is true when the value of the variable *position* controlling the iterations corresponds to either the first or the last iteration. The command is a compound command which causes the process generated by the execution of *IntArrays* to enter break state, and then displays the value of *position* at the console.

The **run** command resumes execution of the process at the statement at which it entered break state. We can make execution resume at a different statement by modifying the value of the current statement pointer, as illustrated in Section 4.5.

5.3.2   Concurrent programs

Let the target program be a concurrent program, and let *P1|*, *P2|*, ..., *Pn|* be the names of the processes generated by the execution of the program. At any given time, the process *Pi|* can be either in run state or in break state (Figure 5.2). The run state is the initial process state.

The **break** simple command makes it possible to switch one or more processes from run state into break state. It has the form

   break <process name>, <process name>, ..., <process name>

This command has no effect on the processes in break state.

The **run** simple command makes it possible to switch one or more processes from break state into run state. This command has the form

   run <process name>, <process name>, ..., <process name>

For each specified process, this command resumes the process elaborations in the block specified by the block pointer of this process, at the statement specified by the statement pointer of this block. This command has no effect on the processes in run state.

The process list in the **break** and **run** commands can be omitted. The meaning of a **break** or **run** command with no process specification will be illustrated shortly.

Example 5.11

Let us refer to the program *Occasions* presented in Chapter 4 (see Figure 4.3), and let *Rep* be an alias for the path name of the block of the process *Reporter*, as defined by the command

alias *Rep* := :*Occasions*:*Reporter*

In the execution of *Occasions*, the directive which follows generates a synchronous break trap to *Reporter* before starting up the update of the array *total*:

[*Rep*$5 ->] **break** *Rep*|

The programmer can now inspect and even alter the state of *Reporter* by means of the **put** and **get** commands. He can then resume

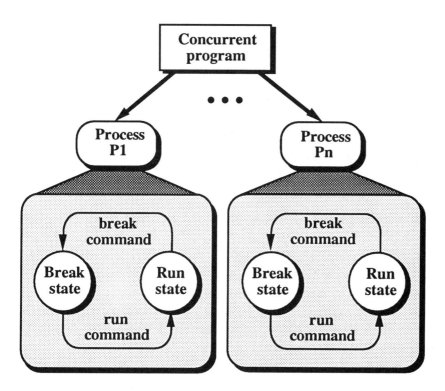

Figure 5.2 The states of the processes generated by the execution of a concurrent program.

the execution of *Reporter* by issuing the command

run *Rep*|

Let us consider a directive specifying an event defined in terms of the activity of a given process *Pi*|. If the command in this directive is a **break** command involving *Pi*| as well as other processes *Pj*|, *Pk*|, ..., then the directive places a break trap which is synchronous for *Pi*| and asynchronous for *Pj*|, *Pk*|, ... The programmer will identify the point reached by the control flow of *Pj*|, *Pk*|, ... when these processes have been suspended by inspecting their current statement pointers.

Example 5.12

In the execution of the program *Occasions*, the simple directive which follows generates a break trap on a near-overflow situation involving the array *total*:

alias *Obs* := :*Occasions*:*Observer*
alias *Rep* := :*Occasions*:*Reporter*
alias *Adc* := :*Occasions*:*Reporter*:*Addocc*
[*Adc*:*t*!W -> *Adc*:*t* [*Adc*:*position*] = (0.9 * *maxint*)] \
        break *Obs*|, *Rep*|

In this directive, the event is defined in terms of a write-mode elementary access to the parameter *t* of the procedure *Addocc* declared in *Reporter*. *Addocc* is called by the statement :*Occasions*:*Reporter*$5. In this call, the actual parameter which is substituted for *t* is the array *total*. The write-mode access will be produced on each iteration of the statement :*Occasions*:*Reporter*:*Addocc*$3. If the value of the element of *total* being processed by the current iteration is equal to 0.9 * *maxint* (a near-overflow situation), the condition specified by the event is satisfied, and the event occurs. A **break** command is now issued, which generates a synchronous trap to *Reporter* and an asynchronous trap to *Observer*. The programmer will identify the point reached by the control flow of *Observer* by inspecting the current statement pointer of this process, for instance, by issuing the command

   rput *Obs*|@

5.3.3   Process groups

In a debugging session involving a complex concurrent program generating a high number of processes, the management of the states of the processes may be simplified by organizing them into *groups*. This result can be obtained by means of the **group** simple command, which has the form

   group <group identifier> := <process name>, <process
       name>, ..., <process name>

This command generates a group consisting of the named processes, and associates the specified identifier with this group. A **group** command involving an existing group alters the definition of this group to contain the named processes. A process may belong to two or more groups at the same time. This result will be obtained by including the name of the process in each of the **group** commands generating these groups.

   The process list in the **break** and **run** commands can include one or more group identifiers. In this case, in the command execution, each group identifier is replaced by the names of the processes included in that group.

   The special group identifier 'ALL' stands for a group which includes all the processes generated by the execution of the target program. Let $P1$|, $P2$|, ... , Pn| be the names of these processes. The command

   break ALL

switches all the processes into break state, thereby suspending their elaborations. It is equivalent to the command

   break $P1$|, $P2$|, ..., Pn|

The command

   run ALL

switches all the processes into run state, thereby resuming their elaborations. It is equivalent to the command

run *P1|, P2|, ... Pn|*

The process list in the **break** and **run** commands can be omitted. In this case, in the command execution, a *default* process group is used. At the beginning of the PDE session, the default group is the group ALL. It can be changed by means of the **default group** simple command, which has the form

default group <group identifier>

Example 5.13

In the program *ConcStmt* presented in Chapter 4 (see Figure 4.2), the command

group *G12* := :*ConcStmt*$3|, :*ConcStmt*$5|

generates a group named *G12* which includes the first and the second process. The command

break *G12*

suspends the elaborations of these two processes.
After issuing the command

default group *G12*

the group *G12* will be the default group. We can now resume execution of the processes in this group by simply issuing the command

run

Existing groups can be removed by means of the **ungroup** command, which has the form

ungroup <group identifier>, <group identifier>, ..., <group identifier>

The **group display** simple command makes it possible to display the names of the processes in the existing groups. This command has the form

group display to <file>

The display is produced in the form of a sequence of characters. The contents of the named file are replaced with this sequence. If the file does not exist, it is created. The file specification can be omitted. In this case, the keyword **to** must also be omitted, and the character sequence is transmitted to the console.

A group display can be appended to a file by issuing a **group display** command with the **append** attribute, as follows:

group display append to <file>

A permanent redirection to a given file of the data output generated by the **group display** command can be obtained by means of the **permanent output** command, introduced in Section 2.7.

Part II

The utilization of a program debugging environment

Contents

Chapter 6

The debugging of sequential programs

Objective

The objective of this chapter is to describe the debugging techniques for sequential programs and to present a number of applications of the PDE command language which support these techniques. The examples are given in the form of solutions to problems frequently encountered in the program-debugging phase.

Contents

6.1 INTRODUCTION

Cyclical debugging is perhaps the debugging method used most widely with sequential programs [McDowell, 1989]. Once the existence of a bug has been revealed, the programmer forms one or more hypotheses about its cause. In this phase, the program is executed with additional test data in order to collect more information concerning the error. The various hypotheses can be derived either by induction, which entails the differences between the unsuccessful and successful test cases, or by deduction: by using a list of possible theoretical causes for the suspected error. In either case, the program should be tested on the simplest input pattern that might prove or disprove each hypothesis. When the bug is located, appropriate corrections are determined and verified by repeating the tests. The process is iterated until a valid solution is found. In order to locate the program error, it may be necessary to systematically exclude parts of the program that have been demonstrated not to contain the bug, thus narrowing down the code portion to be tested. This can be done by examining intermediate results.

Sequential debugging techniques use a *state-based* approach: the state of a sequential program can be characterized simply by the value of the program counter and the memory image of the program data [LeBlanc, 1985]. Such techniques rely heavily on the *reproducible* nature of a sequential program, thanks to which two successive executions of the same program produce identical results provided that we supply the same input data [Kaner, 1988].

6.1.1 Tracing techniques

Debugging techniques can be classified into two categories, *tracing* techniques and *controlled-execution* techniques. Tracing techniques are based on the gathering and recording of portions of given behavioural aspects of the target program at specific execution steps. State and flow traces can be collected, which contain information on the program state history and on the program flow history, respectively. In *automatic* tracing, all changes in values for all variables and all changes in control flow are recorded. In *selective* tracing, the trace gathering is limited to one or more program fragments and/or selected variables. The trace will subsequently be examined in order to discover erroneous sequences of execution states.

The basic mechanism of any trace facility is the trace trap. A *conditional* trace trap is a trace trap generated as a consequence of the occurrence of an event or the violation of an assertion. *Assertions* are logical predicates defined in terms of the state of the program and/or of PDE. As will be shown shortly, conditional trace traps can be used to implement a form of selective tracing. Furthermore, they provide dynamic control over trap generation, i.e., the ability to turn trap generation on or off, without manual intervention, according to the dynamic behaviour of the target program.

6.1.2   Controlled-execution techniques

In controlled-execution techniques, the user monitors the behaviour of the program interactively, by means of break traps. When the process generated by the execution of the program enters the break state, the user examines and possibly alters the state of the elaborations, as well as the layout of the debugging experiment, dynamically. In PDE, a break trap is produced by a directive which includes a break command.

In the following sections we will propose several problems, reflecting a wide set of situations which are likely to occur in practical program-debugging sessions. We will show that PDE encompasses all widely used techniques for debugging sequential programs. This is a consequence of the fact that PDE provides a simple, powerful set of primitives which can be used to adequately support any given debugging experiment.

6.2   TRACING THE VALUES OF A VARIABLE

A directive which specifies an event expressed in terms of one or more target variables can be effectively used to implement a form of selective tracing, by including an output command in that directive aimed at displaying the value of those target entities. By using guarded directives, we can meet an even more stringent requirement, i.e., to limit trace generation to a given program fragment. The following problem shows applications of this type of selective tracing in the acquisition of state traces.

Problem 6.1

Let us refer to the program *ResMgmt*, introduced in Chapter 2 (see Figure 2.1). We want: *(a)* to trace the values assumed by the program variable *rpool*, declared in the main program block; and *(b)* to trace the values assumed by *rpool* in the execution of the function *Get*.

Solution: (a)

$$[:ResMgmt:rpool!W ->] \textbf{ put } :ResMgmt:rpool \qquad (1)$$

On each modification of the value of *rpool*, the **put** command in this directive displays the value of this variable on the console.

(b)

$$
\begin{aligned}
&\textbf{alias } Get := :ResMgmt:Get \\
&\textbf{allocate } TRACING : BOOLEAN \\
&[Get\$1 ->] \ TRACING := TRUE & (1) \\
TRACING \ &[:ResMgmt:rpool!W ->] \backslash & (2) \\
&\quad \textbf{put } :ResMgmt:rpool \\
&[Get\$1!T ->] \ TRACING := FALSE & (3)
\end{aligned}
$$

The first command defines *Get* as an alias for the block path name *:ResMgmt:Get*. The second command allocates the Boolean register TRACING and initializes it to FALSE. Upon the beginning and termination of the execution of the function *Get*, the directives (1) and (3) set and clear the register, thus turning on and off the tracing activity. TRACING is used in directive (2) to control the generation of the trace. On each write access to *rpool*, if TRACING is set, the **put** command in this directive displays the value of the variable on the console.

In the solution of the above problem, we have defined an alias for the absolute block path name of a function. From now on, we will freely use procedure and function names instead of the absolute path names, *implicitly assuming the required alias definitions.*

6.3　TRACING THE EXECUTION OF PROGRAM PORTIONS

The flow history of a program fragment can be expressed in terms of the sequence of all simple and structured statements executed in that fragment. On the other hand, collecting program flow information at a coarser level of granularity, e.g., branches and subprogram calls, is often sufficient to completely describe the flow history of a program fragment. Problems 6.2 and 6.3, which follow, show typical applications of selective tracing techniques in the acquisition of flow histories.

Problem 6.2

In the program *ResMgmt*, we want: *(a)* to display the flow history of the function *Get*; *(b)* to trace the execution of the statements of *Get*; *(c)* to trace the execution of the statements of *Get* when this function is called from inside the program fragment between the statements *:ResMgmt$4* and *:ResMgmt$9*; and *(d)* to trace the execution of the statements in *Get*, as well as the statements in the fragment.

Solution: *(a)*

Of course, statements belonging to the same compound statement are always executed the same number of times. It follows that a flow trace of *Get* can be generated by recording the execution of the statements *Get$1*, *Get$4*, *Get$6* and *Get$7*. This result can be obtained by activating the following directive:

$$[\; Get\$1, \; Get\$4, \; Get\$6, \; Get\$7 \to \;] \; \textbf{rput} \; @ \qquad\qquad (1)$$

(b)

On execution of any statement of the function *Get*, the following directive displays the statement being executed:

$$[\ Get\$1^{**} ->\ ]\ \textbf{rput}\ @ \qquad\qquad (1)$$

(c)

$$
\begin{aligned}
&\textbf{allocate}\ \text{TRACING : BOOLEAN} \\
&[\ :ResMgmt\$4 ->\ ]\ \text{TRACING := TRUE} \qquad (1) \\
\text{TRACING}\quad &[\ Get\$1^{**} ->\ ]\ \textbf{rput}\ @ \qquad\qquad\qquad (2) \\
&[\ :ResMgmt\$5!T ->\ ]\ \text{TRACING := FALSE} \quad (3)
\end{aligned}
$$

The first command allocates the Boolean register TRACING and initializes it to FALSE. TRACING is set and cleared by directives (1) and (3) upon the beginning and the termination of the execution of the fragment, respectively. On execution of any statement of the function *Get*, directive (2) displays the statement being executed. This display is only produced when TRACING is set.

(d)

The solution to this case can easily be derived from the solutions to cases *(b)* and *(c)*, as follows:

$$
\begin{aligned}
&\textbf{allocate}\ \text{TRACING : BOOLEAN} \\
&[\ :ResMgmt\$4 ->\ ]\ \text{TRACING := TRUE} \qquad (1) \\
&[\ :ResMgmt\$5!T ->\ ]\ \text{TRACING := FALSE} \quad (2) \\
\text{TRACING}\quad &[\ ->\ ]\ \textbf{rput}\ @ \qquad\qquad\qquad\qquad (3) \\
&[\ Get\$1^{**} ->\ ]\ \textbf{rput}\ @ \qquad\qquad\qquad (4)
\end{aligned}
$$

Problem 6.3

Trace the calls to the subprograms of the program *ResMgmt*.

Solution:

$$
\begin{aligned}
&[\ Init\$1 ->\ ]\ \textbf{put}\ \text{'Init'},\ Init{:}apool \qquad\qquad\qquad\qquad\quad (1) \\
&[\ Get\$1 ->\ ]\ \textbf{put}\ \text{'Get'},\ Get{:}apool \qquad\qquad\qquad\qquad\quad (2) \\
&[\ IsBusy\$1 ->\ ]\ \textbf{put}\ \text{'IsBusy'},\ IsBusy{:}apool,\ IsBusy{:}rn \quad (3) \\
&[\ Release\$1 ->\ ]\ \textbf{put}\ \text{'Release'},\ Release{:}apool,\ Release{:}rn \ (4)
\end{aligned}
$$

Upon the beginning of the execution of the first statement of the procedure *Init*, directive (1) displays the subprogram name and the values of the subprogram parameters. Similar actions are performed by directives (2) through (4) with respect to the functions *Get* and *IsBusy*, and the procedure *Release*, respectively.

6.4 DETECTING REFERENCES TO UNINITIALIZED VARIABLES

In most programming languages, the value of a variable is not defined before the first assignment to that variable. Therefore, a program performing a read access to the variable before this first assignment occurs is erroneous. The following example shows how we can detect a situation of this type.

Problem 6.4

In the program *ResMgmt*, the following directives detect any read access to the variable *rpool* (declared in the main program block) which occurs before the initialization of this variable:

$$\textbf{allocate } \text{FIRSTW : BOOLEAN}$$

not FIRSTW [:*ResMgmt:rpool*!W ->] \	(1)
FIRSTW := TRUE	
not FIRSTW [:*ResMgmt:rpool*!R ->] **rput** @	(2)

The first command allocates the Boolean register FIRSTW and initializes it to FALSE. On each read access to *rpool*, the command in directive (2) displays the target statement generating that access. On the first write access to *rpool*, the assignment command in directive (1) sets FIRSTW, thus closing both directives (1) and (2). In this way, no display will be generated by directive (2) after the initialization of *rpool*.

6.5 DETECTING NEVER-REFERENCED VARIABLES

An incorrect specification of the condition in a conditional statement may cause an erroneous choice of execution path. One clue to the presence of an error of this type could be the discovery that, on running the program with a given data set, a variable which should be used instead remains unaccessed, as the control path referencing that variable has not been followed.

Problem 6.5

In the program *ResMgmt*, the following directives detect whether the variable *res*, declared in the main program block, remains unreferenced. This erroneous behaviour may be produced if, for instance, the condition in the **if** statement *:ResMgmt$5* is erroneously specified as an equality.

<pre>
          allocate FIRST : BOOLEAN
not FIRST [:ResMgmt:res!RW ->] FIRST := TRUE   (1)
not FIRST [:ResMgmt$1!T ->] \   (2)
          rput 'No access to variable :ResMgmt:res'
</pre>

Upon termination of the execution of the main program block, the **rput** command in directive (2) displays a warning message. On the first read or write access to *res*, the assignment command in directive (1) sets the Boolean register FIRST, thereby closing both directives (1) and (2). In this way, no warning message will be produced after this first access.

6.6 CHECKING CONTROL FLOW CONSTRAINTS

In some situations, whether a given operation in a program can be executed or not depends on the past flow history. By means of events and guards we can check whether given constraints on the sequences of the operations are met.

Problem 6.6

In the program *ResMgmt*, the correct use of the resources in the pool *rpool* imposes a number of constraints on the order in which the operations *Init*, *Get* and *Release* are executed: the pool must be initialized before resources can be obtained from it, and the release of a resource must be preceded by the acquisition of that resource.

The directives which follow detect any erroneous usage of *rpool* by generating a break trap on every attempt to: *(a)* use *rpool* if it has not been initialized; and *(b)* release a free resource.

(a)

> **allocate** IN : BOOLEAN
> [*Init*$1 ->] IN := TRUE   (1)
> **not** IN [:*ResMgmt*:*rpool*!RW ->] **break**   (2)

Directive (2) generates a break trap upon any access to *rpool*. The guard of this directive is expressed in terms of the Boolean register IN. This register is set by directive (1) upon the beginning of the execution of the procedure *Init*. In this way, the break traps are generated only if the access to *rpool* is performed from outside *Init*, when this procedure has not yet been executed.

(b)

> [*Release*$1 -> *Release*:*apool* [*Release*:*rn*] = *free*] **break** (1)

This directive generates a break trap on the beginning of the execution of *Release* if the resource specified by the input parameter *rn* is in the free state.

6.7 STEPWISE EXECUTION

Stepwise execution generates traps periodically. The period can be expressed, for instance, in terms of the number of target statements executed, or the number of accesses made to one or more target entities [Johnson, 1982]. Of course, using stepwise execution to periodically generate trace traps implements a form of selective tracing.

Problem 6.7

With reference to the program *ResMgmt*, the following directives sample the value of the variable *count*, declared in the main program block. The sampling period is expressed in terms of the number of write accesses to *count*.

$$\textbf{allocate } \text{PERIOD, ACCESSES : INTEGER}$$
$$[\ :ResMgmt\$1 \text{ -> }]\ \textbf{rget } \text{PERIOD} \qquad\qquad (1)$$
$$[\ :ResMgmt{:}count!W \text{ -> }]\ \backslash \qquad\qquad\qquad\quad (2)$$
$$\qquad \text{ACCESSES} := \text{ACCESSES} + 1$$
$$\text{ACCESSES} = \text{PERIOD } [\text{ -> }]\ \{ \qquad\qquad\quad (3)$$
$$\qquad \text{ACCESSES} := 0;\ \textbf{put } :ResMgmt{:}count$$
$$\qquad \}$$

The register PERIOD specifies the sampling period, and the register ACCESSES is used as an access counter. When the program execution begins, the **rget** command in directive (1) reads the sampling period from the console and stores it into PERIOD. Directive (2) increases ACCESSES on each modification of *count*. When the value of ACCESSES becomes equal to the sampling period, directive (3) clears ACCESSES and produces the desired display.

6.8 VALUE-RANGE CHECKS

A *value-range check* generates a trap upon the violation of given in-range or out-of-range constraints. A check of this type can be used to monitor the values assumed by a particular target entity, in order to detect a range violation when the specification of range constraints is not supported by the programming language or the compiler, for instance. Value-range checks can also be used to restrict the value range of a certain variable to one which is narrower than that otherwise permitted by the variable type.

In PDE, we can specify a check which generates a trap not only on the first violation of designated range constraints, but also on each subsequent access to the variable involved in the check, independently of the value assumed by the variable at the time of the new access. One application of this technique is to monitor unsafe situations in which the program state is suspected to be close to an error (e.g., near-overflow and near-underflow situations), as illustrated in the following problem.

Problem 6.8

As seen in Section 2.1, the function *Get* of the program *ResMgmt* returns the order number of a free resource in the pool specified by the parameter *apool*. To this aim, *Get* processes the resources of *apool* by means of the **while** statement :*ResMgmt:Get*$3, which uses the local variable *Get:count* to select the resource involved in the current iteration. We say that the allocation of a new resource is *unsafe* when more than 90 per cent of the resources are busy. We want: *(a)* to trace each unsafe allocation within *rpool*; and *(b)* to generate a break trap upon the first unsafe allocation and on each subsequent allocation.

Solution: (a)

$$[\ Get\$8!T \rightarrow Get:count < 0.1*:ResMgmt:last \ ] \setminus \qquad (1)$$
$$\mathbf{put} \ Get:count - 1$$

The event in this directive is expressed in terms of a terminate-mode elementary access to the statement *Get*$8, and a conditional which is true when the value of the variable *Get:count* is less than 0.1*:*ResMgmt:last*. When this event occurs, the directive displays the number of free resources in the pool *Get:apool*.

(b)

$$\mathbf{allocate} \ IN, UNSAFE : BOOLEAN$$
$$[\ Get\$1 \rightarrow] \ IN := TRUE \qquad (1)$$
$$[\ Get\$1!T \rightarrow] \ IN := FALSE \qquad (2)$$
$$IN \ \mathbf{and} \ \mathbf{not} \ UNSAFE \ [:ResMgmt:rpool!W \rightarrow \setminus \qquad (3)$$
$$Get:count < 0.1*:ResMgmt:last \ ] \ \{$$
$$UNSAFE := TRUE$$
$$\mathbf{break}$$
$$\}$$
$$IN \ \mathbf{and} \ UNSAFE \ [:ResMgmt:rpool!W \rightarrow] \ \mathbf{break} \qquad (4)$$

Directives (1) and (2) set and clear the Boolean register IN upon the beginning and the termination of the execution of the function *Get*, respectively. On the first unsafe allocation within the pool *rpool*, directive (3) sets the Boolean register UNSAFE and generates a break trap. A break trap is also generated by directive (4) on each subsequent allocation within this pool.

6.9 MONITORING CONTROL PATHS

Even in a program of moderate size, the possible control paths may be so numerous that it would be hard, if not impossible, to provide test data which exercise all of them. There are a number of reasons for a program fragment not be executed, including programming errors. For instance, the program may be erroneously coded in such a way that all links to a particular fragment are omitted. Furthermore, it may happen that, as a consequence of a program modification, the programmer decides to eliminate a fragment from the program, and so breaks all the links to that fragment, but mistakenly leaves the fragment in place. It follows that it is important to be able to detect whether a given program fragment has been executed or not. Problem 6.9, below, shows the PDE implementation of a debugging experiment of this type.

Problem 6.9

The Pascal program *QueueMgmt*, shown in Figure 6.1, implements queues of integer items which are extracted from the front and inserted at the rear of the queues. The implementation of a queue uses a record containing three fields: an array *items*, each element of which can store a queue item; and two integers f and r, to contain the index of the array element before the front, and of that at the rear of the queue, respectively. The elements of *items* are numbered from 1 up to the value of the program constant *maxqueue*. The array is treated as a circular array, the last element being considered adjacent to the first. We use the conditions $f = r$ and $f = (r \bmod maxqueue) + 1$ to determine whether a queue is empty or full, respectively. This means that a queue is full when only one array element is free.

The function *Search* yields the position of the first item having the value specified by the parameter n in the queue specified by the parameter q. If n is not in q, *Search* returns the value 0. The proce-

```
     {:QueueMgmt}        program QueueMgmt (...);
 {:QueueMgmt:maxqueue}   const maxqueue = ...;
   {:QueueMgmt:index}    type index = 1..maxqueue;
  {:QueueMgmt:index0}       index0 = 0..maxqueue;
  {:QueueMgmt:queue}        queue =   record
                                        items : array [index] of integer;
                                        f, r : index
                                      end;
     {:QueueMgmt:q}      var q : queue;
     {:QueueMgmt:x}          x : integer;
     {:QueueMgmt:C}          C : char;
 {:QueueMgmt:position}       position : index0;
 {:QueueMgmt:Search}    function Search (
 {:QueueMgmt:Search:q}        var q : queue;
 {:QueueMgmt:Search:n}        n : integer
 {:QueueMgmt:Search:Search}   ) : index0;
 {:QueueMgmt:Search:i}        var i : index;
 {:QueueMgmt:Search:found}    found : boolean;
 {:QueueMgmt:Search$1}    begin {Search}
            {$2}            with q do
            {$3}              if f = r
            {$4}              then Search := 0
            {$5}              else   begin
            {$6}                     i := f;
            {$7}                     found := false;
            {$8}                     while (not found) and (i <> r)
            {$9}                     do   begin
            {$10}                       i := (i mod maxqueue) + 1;
            {$11}                       found := items [i] = n
                                      end;
            {$12}                  if found
            {$13}                  then   if i > f
            {$14}                         then Search := i - f
            {$15}                         else Search :=
                                                  i + maxqueue - f
            {$16}                  else Search := 0
                                   end
                             end; {Search}
 {:QueueMgmt:Insert}    procedure Insert (
 {:QueueMgmt:Insert:q}        var q : queue;
 {:QueueMgmt:Insert:n}        n : integer);
 {:QueueMgmt:Insert$1}    begin {Insert}
            {$...}          ...
                         end; {Insert}
```

Figure 6.1   Pascal program *QueueMgmt*.

```
{:QueueMgmt:Remove}      procedure Remove (
{:QueueMgmt:Remove:q}        var q : queue;
{:QueueMgmt:Remove:n}        var n : integer);
{:QueueMgmt:Remove$1}     begin {Remove}
         {$...}               ...
                          end; {Remove}
     {:QueueMgmt:Init}     procedure Init (
     {:QueueMgmt:Init:q}       var q : queue);
     {:QueueMgmt:Init$1}    begin {Init}
              {$2}              q.f := 1;
              {$3}              q.r := 1
                           end; {Init}
 {:QueueMgmt$1}  begin {QueueMgmt}
              {$2}          Init (q);
              {$3}          read (C);
              {$4}          while C in ['S', 'I', 'R']
              {$5}             do  begin
              {$6}                    case C of
              {$7}                    'S' :   begin
              {$8}                                readln (x);
              {$9}                                position := Search (q, x);
             {$10}                                if position > 0
             {$11}                                then writeln (position)
             {$12}                                else writeln ('not found')
                                             end;
             {$13}                    'I' :   begin
             {$14}                                readln (x);
             {$15}                                Insert (q, x)
                                             end;
             {$16}                    'R' :   begin
             {$17}                                readln;
             {$18}                                Remove (q, x)
                                             end
                                          end;
             {$19}                    read (C)
                                   end
                          end. {QueueMgmt}
```

Figure 6.1 *Continued.*

dure *Insert* inserts a new item into the queue specified by the parameter *q*. The value of the new item is specified by the parameter *n*. The procedure *Remove* extracts the item at the front of the queue specified by the parameter q, and returns the value n of this item. Finally, the procedure *Init* initializes the queue specified by the parameter q.

The program body cyclically reads in a character C and performs the operation specified by this character: 'S' for search, 'I' for insertion and 'R' for removal of a queue item. Any other character causes the program to terminate. In the case of a search or an insertion, a subsequent read is used to obtain the value x to be searched for or inserted, respectively.

Of course, the confidence that a program is bug-free increases with the percentage of possible control paths that are executed with the expected results. Now suppose that in the program *QueueMgmt* the sequence of the values of variable C are such that each branch of the **case** statement :*QueueMgmt*$6; contained in the main program body, should be executed at least once. The following directives generate a break trap if the program terminates and one or more branches have not been tried:

> **allocate** S11, S12, S13, S16 : BOOLEAN
> [:*QueueMgmt*$11 ->] S11 := TRUE   (1)
> [:*QueueMgmt*$12 ->] S12 := TRUE   (2)
> [:*QueueMgmt*$13 ->] S13 := TRUE   (3)
> [:*QueueMgmt*$16 ->] S16 := TRUE   (4)
> **not** (S11 **and** S12 **and** S13 **and** S16) \   (5)
>   [:*QueueMgmt*$4!T ->] **break**

At the beginning of the execution of the **then** and the **else** alternatives of the **if** statement :*QueueMgmt*$10, directives (1) and (2) set the Boolean registers S11 and S12. Similar actions are performed by directives (3) and (4) with respect to the statements :*QueueMgmt*$13 and :*QueueMgmt*$16, and with respect to the Boolean registers S13 and S16. Upon the completion of the activities involved in the execution of the **while** statement :*QueueMgmt*$4, directive (5) generates a break trap if any alternative sequence of statements within the **case** statement :*QueueMgmt*$6 has not been executed.

The next problem shows a further application of control path monitoring, i.e., the verification that a given path has actually been followed.

Problem 6.10

In the execution of the program *QueueMgmt*, suppose that the queue contains one or more items. Suppose also that we initially search for a value which is contained only in the first queue item, then we remove this first item, and, finally, we perform a new search for that value. As a consequence of this sequence of operations, the control path should pass through the statements *:QueueMgmt*$11, *:QueueMgmt*$18, and *:QueueMgmt*$12, in that order. The following directives can be used to generate a break trap when the control path has passed through these three statements in sequence:

$$[:QueueMgmt\$11 ->] A\%B := TRUE \qquad (1)$$
$$A\%B \quad [:QueueMgmt\$18 ->] B\%B := TRUE \qquad (2)$$
$$B\%B \quad [:QueueMgmt\$12!T ->] \textbf{break} \qquad (3)$$

Of course, this sequence of directives can be easily extended to treat control paths expressed in terms of an arbitrarily large number of statements.

6.10 ACCUMULATED TRAPS

In the execution of a loop, more iterations than expected may be a symptom of error, for instance, an incorrect or incomplete specification of the expression controlling the iterations. A situation of this type can be detected by using an *accumulated trap*, i.e., a trap which is triggered by the *n*th occurrence of a given event. The following problem shows an application of this technique.

Problem 6.11

In the program *QueueMgmt*, suppose that the value of the program constant *maxqueue* is 10. Suppose also that the function *Search* has been implemented as illustrated in Figure 6.2. In this erroneous im-

```
{:QueueMgmt:Search}        function Search (
{:QueueMgmt:Search:q}          var q : queue;
{:QueueMgmt:Search:n}          n : integer
{:QueueMgmt:Search:Search}     ) : index0;
{:QueueMgmt:Search:i}          var i : index;
{:QueueMgmt:Search:found}      found : boolean;
{:QueueMgmt:Search$1}      begin {Search}
              {$2}         with q do
              {$3}           if f = r
              {$4}           then Search := 0
              {$5}           else   begin
              {$6}                     i := f;
              {$7}                     found := false;
              {$8}                     while not found
                                               {incomplete condition}
              {$9}                     do   begin
              {$10}                             i := (i mod maxqueue) + 1;
              {$11}                             found := items [i] = n
                                             end;
              {$12}                     if found
              {$13}                     then   if i > f
              {$14}                            then Search := i - f
              {$15}                            else Search :=
                                                        i + maxqueue - f
              {$16}                     else Search := 0
                                   end
                       end; {Search}
```

Figure 6.2 An incorrect implementation of the function *Search*.

plementation, the **while** statement *Search*$8 is exited when the element sought is found; however, if the desired element is not contained in the array, the loop does not terminate. This is a consequence of the incomplete specification of the condition controlling the iterations.

   In order to detect an error of this type, we will generate a break trap after ten iterations of the **while** statement *Search*$8, i.e., when all the elements of the array *items* have been processed. This result can be obtained as follows:

allocate COUNT : INTEGER
[*Search*$9 ->] \   (1)
   switch

```
    case COUNT < 10 :
        COUNT := COUNT + 1
    case TRUE :
        break
    end switch
```

The integer register COUNT is used as an event counter. On each execution of the statement *Search*$9, which forms the body of the **while** statement *Search*$8, directive (1) increases the value of COUNT. After the 10th iteration, this same directive generates a break trap.

In the erroneous version of the function *Search* shown in Figure 6.2, the number sought by *Search* will also be compared with the unused components of the array. It follows that this function might return a non-null position for an integer which is not, in fact, present in the queue. This situation can be detected by an application of value-range checks, by checking whether the value returned by *Search* lies between the values of the indexes of the first and the last items of the queue, as follows:

alias $S := :QueueMgmt:Search$
[S1!T -> ((S:q.f< S:q.r)$ **and** \   (1)
   $((S:Search <= S:q.f)$ **or** $(S:Search > S:q.r)))$ \
  or $((S:q.f > S:q.r)$ **and** \
   $((S:q.r < S:Search)$ **and** $(S:Search <= S:q.f)))$] **break**

As a consequence of the fact that the array is treated as a circular array, it may well be the case that the element at the front of the queue follows that at the queue's rear. The conditional in directive (1) takes this case into account. Upon the termination of the execution of the function *Search*, the **break** command in this directive generates a break trap if the value returned by *Search* references an unused element of the array.

6.11 SINGLE STEPPING

As seen in Section 1.1, *single stepping* is the ability to execute one statement of source code at a time. In many debugging environments, single stepping through a program fragment requires heavy manual intervention from the user. Typically, the user inserts a break trap at the beginning of the fragment; when this trap is encountered, he will repeatedly ask for the execution of a single statement, until the end of the fragment is reached. More sophisticated environments allow the user to ask for the single-step execution of a certain number of statements by means of a single command. Even in an environment of this type, the amount of manual intervention required from the user may be exceedingly time-consuming; consider the case in which the fragment under scrutiny is inside a loop, for instance. With PDE, on the other hand, the user can single-step one or more fragments, with no manual intervention even for iterated executions.

Problem 6.12

Single-step the execution of the program fragment between the statements *Search*$8 and *Search*$16 of the function *Search* of the program *QueueMgmt*.

Solution:

$$\text{allocate SSTEP : BOOLEAN}$$

	[*Search*$8 ->] SSTEP := TRUE	(1)
SSTEP	[*Search*$1** ->] **break**	(2)
	[*Search*$12!T ->] SSTEP := FALSE	(3)

Directive (2) generates a break trap upon the beginning of the execution of every statement of the function *Search*. The guard of this directive is expressed in terms of the Boolean register SSTEP. This register is set on the beginning of the execution of the first statement, and cleared on the termination of the execution of the last statement of the fragment. In this way, break trap generation is limited to the statements of the fragment.

6.12 DETECTING LOOPING SITUATIONS

In Problem 6.11, we considered the case of a loop with an incomplete specification of the condition controlling termination of the iterations. This is only one example from the possible reasons for a loop not to terminate. Other examples include a condition whose value is never modified inside the loop. Problem 6.13, which follows, illustrates this situation.

Problem 6.13

Let us consider the following program fragment:

$$\{:P\$10\} \quad \textbf{while } x < 100$$
$$\{\$11\} \quad \textbf{do } ...;$$
$$\{\$...\} \quad ...$$

The condition controlling the termination of the **while** statement $:P\$10$ is expressed in terms of the program variable x. Suppose that the specification of the body of the **while** statement is such that the value of x should be modified at every iteration. We want to generate a break trap if any iteration does not change this value.

Solution:

$$\textbf{allocate} \text{ MODIFIED, CHECK : BOOLEAN}$$
$$[:P\$10 ->] \text{ CHECK := TRUE} \qquad (1)$$
$$[:P\$11 ->] \text{ MODIFIED := FALSE} \qquad (2)$$
$$\text{CHECK } [:P:x!W ->] \text{ MODIFIED := TRUE} \qquad (3)$$
$$\textbf{not} \text{ MODIFIED } [:P\$11!T ->] \textbf{ break} \qquad (4)$$
$$[:P\$10!T ->] \text{ CHECK := FALSE} \qquad (5)$$

Directive (2) clears the Boolean register MODIFIED upon the beginning of the execution of the statement $:P\$11$, which forms the body of the **while** statement $:P\$10$. Directive (3) sets this register upon every write access to variable x. The guard of this directive is expressed in terms of the Boolean register CHECK, which is set and cleared by directives (1) and (5) upon the beginning and the termination, respectively, of the execution of the **while** statement. In this way, MODIFIED is set only if the write access to x is performed inside the **while** statement. Because the guard of directive (4) is expressed in terms of MODIFIED, this directive generates a trap upon the termination of any iteration which has not changed the value of x.

6.13 ACCESS-MODE CHECKS

The detection of violations of access mode constraints (e.g., a write access to a read-only data item) has been recognized as an important means for revealing semantic errors, such as attempts to write into code areas [Lazzerini, 86], [Lopriore, 84]. *Access mode checks* are aimed at the detection of access violations. A check of this type monitors the accesses made to a given target entity and generates traps upon any such violation.

PDE allows us to implement access mode checks by specifying an access mode for a particular data item, and associating that access mode with a designated program fragment (e.g., the body of a sub-program), as illustrated by the following problem.

Problem 6.14

Let us refer again to the program *QueueMgmt*, shown in Figure 6.1. For increased efficiency, the parameter q is transmitted to the function *Search* by reference; however this function must not perform any write access to q. We can detect any such access by causing the access to generate a break trap. This result can be obtained by activating the directive which follows:

$$[\; Search{:}q!W \rightarrow \;] \; \textbf{break} \qquad\qquad (1)$$

Chapter 7

The debugging of shared-variable concurrent programs

Objective

This chapter considers the concurrent programming languages using shared variables for interprocess communication. The syntactic notations for expressing concurrent execution are summarized, and the process synchronization primitives based on shared variables are presented. Then, the outstanding techniques for the debugging of shared-variable concurrent programs are illustrated. Finally, solutions are proposed to a number of common programming errors, including synchronization and timing errors, and deadlock-prone coding.

Contents

7.1   INTRODUCTION

A *concurrent program* consists of a set of sequential processes whose execution can overlap in time, i.e., a process can begin its execution before a previously started process has terminated [Ghezzi, 1987]. The processes may be multiprogrammed on the same processor, or they may be executed in parallel on different processors. They can be either *independent* or *interacting*, and interactions may take place for:

- *competition*, to obtain exclusive access to shared resources; and
- *cooperation*, to exchange information and achieve a common goal.

Competition imposes *mutual exclusion* on attempts to access shared resources. For instance, one process must not be allowed to alter the value of a shared variable while another process is examining this variable. Cooperation places precedence constraints on the sequences of operations performed by the concurrent processes. For example, if a process has to use some data produced by another process, the former must wait for the latter to produce those data.

Interprocess communications may occur via *shared variables* and *message passing* [Andrews, 1983], [Wilson, 1988]. In a shared-variable environment, processes access a common memory. Therefore, both competition and cooperation can take place. In a message-passing environment, however, processes do not share memory. Instead, interprocess communication is achieved through the sending and receipt of messages. Messages are also used for process synchronization, and cooperation is the only kind of process interaction possible.

Concurrent programming languages provide constructs for denoting concurrent execution and expressing interprocess interactions. In this chapter, we will only be concerned with shared-variable concurrent languages. Message-passing languages will be considered in Chapter 8.

7.1.1   Specifying concurrent execution

As seen in Section 4.2, several notations have been proposed for expressing concurrent execution. An example is the **cobegin-coend** statement, which has the form

> **cobegin**
>   <statement>;
>   <statement>;
>   ...;
>   <statement>
> **coend**

This statement activates one process for each of its component statements. These processes proceed concurrently. When all of them terminate, the execution of the **cobegin-coend** statement terminates. For this reason, **coend** is a synchronization point.

An alternative way to express concurrent execution is by means of process declarations. As illustrated in Section 4.2, one possible notation for a process declaration is the following:

> **process** <process identifier>;
>   ... {declaration part}
> **begin**
>   ... {statement part}
> **end**

The declaration part contains the local variables, and the statement part specifies the statements to be executed by the process.

7.1.2   Process creation, activation and termination

Process creation can be either *static* or *dynamic*. A number of concurrent programming languages, e.g., Concurrent Pascal [Brinch Hansen, 1975], permit only the static creation of processes. In a language of this type, a process cannot contain the declaration of other processes; instead, all processes must be declared in the main program block. All the processes which compose a program are activated on the beginning of the program execution. A program is therefore equivalent to a single **cobegin-coend** statement whose component statements are the body of the main program and the body of each declared process.

Other concurrent programming languages, e.g., Ada [ANSI, 1983], permit the dynamic creation and termination of processes. In these languages, process declarations can be nested. A process is created when its declaration is elaborated, and this can occur in any phase of the execution of the program. Process activation can be *explicit*: a process is activated by means of an *ad hoc* statement, or *implicit*: the execution of a process starts up automatically on the beginning of the execution of the block containing the declaration of that process. If activation is implicit, a block containing the declarations of processes $P1$, $P2$, ..., Pn is equivalent to a **cobegin-coend** statement whose component statements are the body of that block and the body of each of the processes $P1$, $P2$, ..., Pn.

7.2 SYNCHRONIZATION PRIMITIVES BASED ON SHARED VARIABLES

As seen in Section 7.1, in a shared-variable concurrent program, processes can both compete for access to shared variables, and cooperate by exchanging information via shared variables. Mutual exclusion can be obtained by means of critical sections. A *critical section* is a sequence of statements which must be executed as an indivisible operation [Andrews, 1983]. If every access to a shared variable is performed within a critical section, only one process at a time can reference that variable: any other process wishing to use the variable will be delayed.

Critical sections can be implemented by using semaphores. A *semaphore* is an integer-valued variable on which two operations are defined, the P and V operations [Silberschatz, 1991]. Let s denote a semaphore. A possible definition of the P operation is as follows:

$s := s - 1;$
if $s < 0$ **then** {suspend}

If the new value of s is less than 0, the process executing the operation is suspended. This process is inserted into a list of waiting processes, which is associated with the semaphore.

The V operation is as follows:

$s := s + 1;$
if $s <= 0$ **then** {resume}

If the new value of s is less than or equal to 0, a waiting process is extracted from the list associated with the semaphore, and the execution of this process is resumed.

P and V are atomic operations. If two or more processes issue these operations on the same semaphore at the same time, the operations will be executed sequentially, in some arbitrary order. Mutual exclusion in accessing a shared resource can be obtained by associating a semaphore with the resource. This semaphore will be initialized to 1. Each critical section will be preceded and followed by a P and a V operation, respectively.

Semaphores can also be used to coordinate the activities of communicating processes. A P operation on a semaphore will be used to suspend a process attempting to perform an action on a shared resource, if the resource state is inappropriate for executing that action. A V operation on the same semaphore will be executed by a process changing the state of the resource, if the new state is compatible with the execution of the suspended process. For example, a process attempting to extract information from an empty buffer will be suspended by a P operation on a semaphore associated with the empty-buffer condition. The execution of this process will be resumed once some other process puts data into the buffer. This latter process will execute a V operation on the semaphore.

Semaphores are powerful but low-level mechanisms, and their use leads to programs which are difficult to understand. Synchronization errors due to misplaced P's and V's are hard to find, as these operations may be disseminated throughout the program. To overcome these drawbacks, higher-level mechanisms for expressing interprocess interactions have been devised. An example is the *monitor* programming language construct [Brinch Hansen, 1973], [Hoare, 1974].

Syntactically, a monitor consists of a heading, a declaration part and a statement part, as follows:

type <monitor identifier> = **monitor**
   ... {declaration part}
begin
   ... {statement part}
end

The heading gives the monitor identifier. The declaration part contains the declaration of the so-called *permanent* variables, and of the procedures which operate on these variables. Finally, the statement part contains the statements aimed at initializing the permanent variables. The monitor procedures can be either *local* or *exported*. The local procedures can only be used inside the monitor. This is not the case for the exported procedures, whose declarations start with the keywords **procedure entry**.

The declaration of an instance of a monitor has the form of a variable declaration:

var <instance identifier> : <monitor identifier>;

An exported procedure is invoked by using the instance identifier and a procedure call, separated by a dot, as follows:

<instance identifier>.<procedure identifier> (<actual parameters>)

A monitor implements the abstract type of a shared resource. The internal representation of the resource is stored in the permanent variables, and the operations for manipulating the resource are concretized by the exported procedures. At any given time, there can be at most one process actively executing one of these procedures. It follows that mutual exclusion in accessing the shared resource implemented by a given monitor instance is guaranteed by the semantics of the monitor construct. On the other hand, cooperation in using the resource must be programmed explicitly, by using an additional mechanism, for instance, variables of the type *condition* [Hoare, 1974].

Only two operations, *wait* and *signal*, are defined on a condition variable [Andrews, 1983]. Execution of the operation *cond.wait*

on the condition variable *cond* suspends the process executing the operation. This process loses exclusive access to the monitor. Execution of the operation

cond.signal .

allows one process suspended on condition *cond* to proceed. If no process is suspended on *cond*, the operation has no other effect.

7.3 DEBUGGING APPROACHES

A possible approach to concurrent-program debugging is to consider each individual process in isolation, and use sequential-program debugging techniques, e.g., controlled-execution techniques and tracing techniques, to discover errors within that process. However, the multi-process composition of concurrent programs is, in itself, a potential source of new classes of errors, and, in particular, interprocess communication and synchronization errors [Garcia-Molina, 1984].

Let us first consider controlled-execution techniques. In the debugging of a concurrent program, an essential feature of the trap-generating mechanism is the ability to generate a break trap on the occurrence of any interprocess interaction. Moreover, we must be allowed to restrict the trap to any subset of the set of processes which compose the program.

As far as the use of tracing techniques with concurrent programs is concerned, the problems connected with the memory space needed to keep the trace and the execution time required to gather the trace are compounded by the fact that we must record the activity of several processes. Keeping a copy of the whole program state and/or flow history may be impractical, and is usually unnecessary; therefore, the use of some form of selective tracing is almost always mandatory [Garcia-Molina, 1984]. A possible approach considers the process as the unit of selective tracing, and records the activity of only a subset of the processes which constitute the concurrent program [Gait, 1985]. In a different approach, one might collect information relevant to only a few aspects of the program activity, e.g., interprocess synchronization.

As stated in Section 1.1, the behaviour of a concurrent program is not reproducible, and different results may be produced when the program is rerun, even in the same environment and with the same input data [LeBlanc, 1987]. A process which is a constituent of a concurrent program alternates its activity between local computations and interprocess interactions. Between any two successive interaction points, constituent processes are independent. The result of a specific execution of the program with given input data is determined by the program *replay trace*, which is the sequence of the process interactions and the data values associated with these interactions. In a shared-variable environment, these data values will be contained in the shared variables; in a message-passing system, they will be contained in the messages exchanged between the processes.

A *cyclical* debugging experiment is an experiment using replay traces to drive the replay of the execution of either the entire program or a subset of the processes which make up the program. A cyclical experiment will consist of a *monitoring* phase, during which we collect the replay trace, and one or more *replay* phases. During a replay phase, the program is rerun with the same input data, and the contents of the replay trace are used to drive the nonsequential aspects of the program execution, e.g., any non-deterministic selections. For instance, we can run a single process by using the replay trace to simulate the other processes of the concurrent program. In each replay, the execution of individual processes will be monitored using sequential-program debugging techniques.

In the rest of this chapter, we will show typical applications of the PDE command language in the implementation of tracing and controlled-execution techniques for the debugging of shared-variable concurrent programs.

7.4 TRACING EVENT HISTORIES

In the previous section, we have stressed the importance of selective tracing in concurrent-program debugging. In this section, with reference to an example of a shared-variable concurrent program, we will present typical applications of these techniques in the monitoring of interprocess interactions as well as in the monitoring of the activities of a single process.

Problem 7.1

The program *Sharing* shown in Figure 7.1 is written in a shared-variable concurrent language specifying concurrent execution by means of process declarations, and using semaphores for process synchronization. This program defines three processes, called *Increaser*, *Decreaser* and *Consumer*. The three processes share access to the variable *shared*. Mutual exclusion in the usage of *shared* is obtained by using a semaphore *mutex*, initialized to 1. *Increaser* adds the value of its local variable *inc* to *shared*. *Decreaser* evaluates the difference between the values of *shared* and of its local variable *dec*. If this difference is greater than the value of the program constant *lowerbound*, the difference is assigned to *shared*; otherwise, *shared* is set to *lowerbound*. *Consumer* reads the value contained in *shared* and sets *shared* to *lowerbound*. It follows that the value obtained by *Consumer* is always greater than or equal to *lowerbound*.

With reference to the program *Sharing*, *(a)* trace each value assigned to *shared*; *(b)* trace each value assigned to *shared* and the name of the process performing the assignment; and *(c)* trace the path followed by the control flow of the process *Increaser* at the level of the write accesses to the local variable *inc* and the global variable *shared*.

Solution: (a)

[:*Sharing*:*shared*!W ->] **put** :*Sharing*:*shared*   (1)

On each modification of *shared*, this directive displays the new value of the variable on the console.

(b)

alias *Increaser* := :*Sharing*:*Increaser*
alias *Decreaser* := :*Sharing*:*Decreaser*
alias *Consumer* := :*Sharing*:*Consumer*
[*Increaser*$5!T ->] **put** 'Increaser', :*Sharing*:*shared*   (1)

```
          {:Sharing}  program Sharing;
  {:Sharing:lowerbound}    const lowerbound = ...;
      {:Sharing:posint}    type posint = 1..maxint;
      {:Sharing:shared}    var shared : posint := lowerbound;
       {:Sharing:mutex}      mutex : semaphore := 1;
   {:Sharing:Increaser}    process Increaser;
{:Sharing:Increaser:inc}     var inc : posint;
  {:Sharing:Increaser$1}    begin {Increaser}
                  {$2}      repeat
                  {$3}        ...; {produce a positive integer
                                     and assign it to inc}
                  {$4}        P (mutex);
                  {$5}        shared := shared + inc;
                  {$6}        V (mutex)
                            until false
                          end; {Increaser}
   {:Sharing:Decreaser}    process Decreaser;
{:Sharing:Decreaser:dec}     var dec : posint;
  {:Sharing:Decreaser$1}    begin {Decreaser}
                  {$2}      repeat
                  {$3}        ...; {produce a positive integer
                                     and assign it to dec}
                  {$4}        P (mutex);
                  {$5}        if shared - dec > lowerbound
                  {$6}        then shared := shared - dec
                  {$7}        else shared := lowerbound;
                  {$8}        V (mutex)
                            until false
                          end; {Decreaser}
    {:Sharing:Consumer}    process Consumer;
{:Sharing:Consumer:consvalue}  var consvalue : posint;
   {:Sharing:Consumer$1}    begin {Consumer}
                  {$2}      repeat
                  {$3}        P (mutex);
                  {$4}        consvalue := shared;
                  {$5}        shared := lowerbound;
                  {$6}        V (mutex);
                  {$7}        ... {use consvalue}
                            until false
                          end; {Consumer}

                          end. {Sharing}
```

Figure 7.1 Concurrent program *Sharing*.

[*Decreaser*$6!T, *Decreaser*$7!T ->] \   (2)
   put 'Decreaser', :*Sharing*:*shared*
[*Consumer*$5!T ->] **put** 'Consumer', :*Sharing*:*shared*   (3)

The first three commands define *Increaser*, *Decreaser* and *Consumer* as aliases for the block path names :*Sharing*:*Increaser*, :*Sharing*:*Decreaser* and :*Sharing*:*Consumer*, respectively. On each write access to the shared variable *shared*, directives (1) through (3) produce the desired display.

(c)

   alias *Increaser* := :*Sharing*:*Increaser*
   [*Increaser*:*inc*!W ->] **rput** *Increaser*|@   (1)
   [*Increaser*$5!T ->] **rput** *Increaser*|@   (2)

On each write access to the local variable *inc*, the **rput** command in directive (1) displays the value of the current statement pointer of *Increaser*. A similar action is performed by directive (2) on termination of the execution of the statement :*Sharing*:*Increaser*$5, i.e., on each modification of the shared variable *shared* performed by *Increaser*.

In the solution of the problem above, we have defined aliases for the process block path names. From now on, we will freely use the process identifiers instead of the process block path names, implicitly assuming the required alias definitions. (In Chapter 6, we made a similar assumption for subprogram names.)

Problem 7.2

The program *ResAlloc* given in Figure 7.2 is written in a concurrent language featuring the monitor construct. The program defines two processes *P1* and *P2*, which share access to an instance *apool* of the monitor *rpool*. This monitor implements a dynamic allocation of a pool of identical resources, which are numbered from 1 to the value of the program constant *N*. The array *free* of *N* Boolean elements represents the state of the resources: the *i*th element of the array has the value *true* if the *i*th resource of the pool is free, and *false* otherwise. The monitor exports two procedures, called *Request* and *Release*, which make it possible to acquire and to release (after use) a resource, respectively. *Request* returns the number i of a free resource, switches this resource to the busy state, and then increases the value of the permanent variable *alloc*, equal to the number of resources allocated. If no resource is free, the requesting process is delayed by a *wait* operation on the condition variable *avail*. *Release* releases the resource whose sequence number is specified by the input parameter i. The resource is switched to the free state, and the value of the variable *alloc* is decreased. The releasing process executes a *signal* operation on *avail*, thus resuming a requesting process previously delayed by the execution of a *wait* operation on this condition variable. The initialization statements of the monitor free all the resources of the pool, and set the number of resources allocated to 0.

With reference to the program *ResAlloc*, the following directives trace the calls made by the processes *P1* and *P2* to the procedures of the monitor:

```
[ Request$1 -> ] \                          (1)
    switch
      case P1|@ = Request$1 :
        put 'P1, Request'
      case P2|@ = Request$1 :
        put 'P2, Request'
    end switch
[ Release$1 -> ] \                          (2)
    switch
      case P1|@ = Release$1 :
        put 'P1, Release'
      case P2|@ = Release$1 :
        put 'P2, Release'
    end switch
```

Each time a process begins execution of the monitor procedure *Request*, directive (1) displays the name of that process, and the name of the procedure, *Request*. Similar actions are performed by directive (2) with respect to the monitor procedure *Release*.

```
        {:ResAlloc}  program ResAlloc;
      {:ResAlloc:N}     const N = ...;
 {:ResAlloc:resnum}     type resnum = 1..N;
  {:ResAlloc:rpool }     rpool = monitor
{:ResAlloc:rpool:free}      var free : array [resnum]
                                of boolean;
{:ResAlloc:rpool:alloc}     alloc : 0..N;
   {:ResAlloc:rpool:i}      i : resnum;
{:ResAlloc:rpool:avail}     avail : condition;
{:ResAlloc:rpool:Request}   procedure entry Request (
{:ResAlloc:rpool:Request:i}    var i : resnum);
{:ResAlloc:rpool:Request$1}  begin {Request}
                {$2}          if alloc = N
                {$3}          then avail.wait;
                {$4}          i := 1;
                {$5}          while not free [i]
                {$6}          do i := i + 1;
                {$7}          free [i] := false;
                {$8}          alloc := alloc + 1
                             end; {Request}
{:ResAlloc:rpool:Release}   procedure entry Release (
{:ResAlloc:rpool:Release:i}    i : resnum);
{:ResAlloc:rpool:Release$1}  begin {Release}
                {$2}          free [i] := true;
                {$3}          alloc := alloc - 1;
                {$4}          avail.signal
                             end; {Release}
 {:ResAlloc:rpool$1}         begin {rpool}
                {$2}          for i := 1 to N
                {$3}          do free [i] := true;
                {$4}          alloc := 0
                             end; {rpool}
 {:ResAlloc:apool}          var apool : rpool;

   {:ResAlloc:P1}          process P1;
  {:ResAlloc:P1:h}            var h : resnum;
 {:ResAlloc:P1$1}          begin {P1}
                {$2}          ...;
                {$3}          apool.Request (h);
                {$4}          ...; {use the hth resource}
                {$5}          apool.Release (h);
                {$6}          ...
                             end; {P1}
```

Figure 7.2 Concurrent program *ResAlloc*.

```
{:ResAlloc:P2}        process P2;
{:ResAlloc:P2:h}         var h : resnum;
{:ResAlloc:P2$1}      begin {P2}
       {$2}              ...;
       {$3}              apool.Request (h);
       {$4}              ...; {use the hth resource}
       {$5}              apool.Release (h);
       {$6}              ...
                       end; {P2}

                     end. {ResAlloc}
```

Figure 7.2 *Continued.*

7.5 CONDITIONAL BREAK TRAPS

An interesting application of conditional break traps is to suspend the execution of all the processes which compose a concurrent program when the program state is suspected to be close to an error, and then selectively advance the computation of only a subset of these processes. In this context, one can profitably apply the PDE capability of organizing processes into groups, so that the programmer can easily direct debugging commands to the processes in a specific group [McDowell, 1989].

Problem 7.3

In the program *Sharing* shown in Figure 7.1, the value of the variable *shared* should never become less than that of the constant *lowerbound*. However, this condition might be violated as a result of programming errors, for instance, if the statement *:Sharing:Increaser*$5 were erroneously coded to decrease, instead of increase, the value of *shared*. In this case, the following directive will switch all processes of the program into break state:

$$[:Sharing:shared!W \to \backslash \qquad (1)$$
$$:Sharing:shared < :Sharing:lowerbound] \textbf{ break } ALL$$

Problem 7.4

In the program *ResAlloc* given in Figure 7.2, a call to the monitor procedure *Release* is erroneous if the value of the parameter *i* corresponds to a free resource. This error might occur, for instance, if a given resource were erroneously released before being requested. An error of this type is detected by the directive

```
[ Release$1 -> :ResAlloc:apool:free [Release:i] ] \              (1)
  switch
    case P1|@ = Release$1 :
      break P1|
    case P2|@ = Release$1 :
      break P2|
  end switch
```

Upon the beginning of the execution of *Release*, if the value of the *i*th element of the array *free* is *true*, this directive generates a break trap to the process executing the procedure.

7.6   DETECTING MISPLACEMENT OF SYNCHRONIZATION PRIMITIVES

A typical error in an implementation of mutual exclusion using semaphores is to protect only a portion of the critical section, instead of the critical section itself [Gait, 1985]. The following problem is concerned with the detection of an error of this type.

Problem 7.5

In the program *Sharing*, suppose that the process *Decreaser* has been erroneously implemented as shown in Figure 7.3. Suppose also that, in this version of the program, *Decreaser* reads the value of *shared* and then *Consumer* modifies this value before *Decreaser* has acquired control of the critical section. This sequence of operations will produce erroneous results if the initial value of *shared* is greater than the quantity *lowerbound* + *dec*. In this case, *Decreaser* will set *shared* to a value which is less than that of *lowerbound*. It

```
{:Sharing:Decreaser}       process Decreaser;
{:Sharing:Decreaser.dec}      var dec : posint;
{:Sharing:Decreaser$1}     begin {Decreaser}
{$2}                          repeat
{$3}                             ...; {produce a positive integer
                                       and assign it to dec}
{$4}                             if shared - dec > lowerbound
{$5}                             then  begin
{$6}                                      P (mutex);
{$7}                                      shared := shared - dec;
{$8}                                      V (mutex)
                                       end
{$9}                             else  begin
{$10}                                     P (mutex);
{$11}                                     shared := lowerbound;
{$12}                                     V (mutex)
                                       end
                                until false
                             end; {Decreaser}
```

Figure 7.3 An erroneous solution to a mutual exclusion problem.

should be noted that the error may well produce no visible effect, as would be the case if, for instance, *Increaser* assigned *shared* a value greater than that of *lowerbound*. However, the error can be made evident by tracing the values assumed by *shared*, as shown in Problem 7.1(*a*), or by using a form of value-range checks and generating a break trap when *shared* assumes a value which is less than that of *lowerbound*, as illustrated in Problem 7.3.

7.7   DETECTING DEADLOCK SITUATIONS

A *deadlock* is a circular wait condition in which every member of a process set has obtained exclusive access to a shared resource, but needs an additional resource which is allocated to the next member of the set [Silberschatz, 1991].

Deadlock problems may arise as a consequence of programming errors. Of course, the capability of detecting and recovering from a deadlock situation without closing the debugging session is particularly attractive. For instance, by switching the deadlocked processes into break state, the programmer can modify the state of one or more of them, thus eliminating the deadlock. He can then resume execution of all the processes, and observe the effects of the modifications made [Griffin, 1988].

The programmer can detect a deadlock state by tracing the execution of each concurrent process. Whenever a process remains suspended for too long on a statement which is a synchronization point, a deadlock should be suspected.

In a different approach, a potential deadlock situation can be revealed through the inspection of the usage of synchronization primitives. This approach is illustrated by the solution to the following problem.

Problem 7.6

Once again, suppose that the process *Decreaser* of the program *Sharing* has been coded erroneously. The version we are presently considering is that shown in Figure 7.4. In this version, a deadlock may occur, for instance, on commencing execution of the **if** state-

```
{:Sharing:Decreaser}      process Decreaser;
{:Sharing:Decreaser.dec}     var dec : posint;
{:Sharing:Decreaser$1}    begin {Decreaser}
{$2}          repeat
{$3}             ...; {produce a positive integer
                          and assign it to dec}
{$4}             P (mutex);
{$5}             if shared - dec > lowerbound
{$6}             then  begin
{$7}                      shared := shared - dec;
{$8}                      V (mutex)
                       end
{$9}             else   shared := lowerbound
                 until false
              end; {Decreaser}
```

Figure 7.4 A misplaced synchronization primitive which may cause a deadlock.

ment :*Sharing*:*Decreaser*$5, if the evaluation of the condition in this statement yields *false*. In this case, *Decreaser* would not execute the *V* operation on the semaphore *mutex*. It follows that, from then on, no process would ever be able to access the variable *shared*.

The following directives detect the occurrence of the situation described above:

allocate FLAG : BOOLEAN
[*Decreaser*$4 ->] \   (1)
  switch
    case FLAG :
      break ALL; **rput** 'Deadlock detected'
    case TRUE :
      FLAG := TRUE
  end switch
[*Decreaser*$8!T ->] FLAG := FALSE   (2)

On the completion of a *V* operation on the semaphore *mutex* by the process *Decreaser*, directive (2) clears the Boolean register FLAG. On the beginning of the execution of the statement :*Sharing*:*Decreaser*$4, directive (1) generates a break trap to all processes or, if FLAG is cleared, it sets FLAG.

7.8 REPLAYING PROGRAM EXECUTION

In Section 7.3, we analysed the utilization of replay traces in the implementation of cyclical debugging experiments. In this section, we will show an application of the PDE command language in an experiment of this type.

Problem 7.7

The execution of the program *Sharing* is characterized by the sequence of the *P* operations on the shared semaphore *mutex*. In order to record this sequence, let us associate a one-character identifier with each of the three processes, *Increaser*, *Decreaser* and *Consumer*, which form the program. On the termination of every *P* op-

eration, we append the identifier of the process which has performed the operation to a trace file, called TRACE, as follows:

[*Increaser*$4!T ->] **rput 'I' append to** TRACE   (1)
[*Decreaser*$4!T ->] **rput 'D' append to** TRACE   (2)
[*Consumer*$3!T ->] **rput 'C' append to** TRACE   (3)

The sequence of synchronization operations can now be repro-
duced by associating a flag with each process, and allowing a process to execute a *P* operation on the semaphore *mutex* only if its flag
is set. We read a process identifier from the file TRACE, and set the
flag associated with the process having that identifier. On termination of the execution of a *V* operation, we clear the flag associated
with the process which has performed this operation. These actions
will be accomplished by activating the following directives:

     allocate FI, FD, FC, ST : BOOLEAN
     allocate PID : CHARACTER
not ST [*Increaser*$1, *Decreaser*$1, *Consumer*$1 ->] { (1)
     ST := TRUE; **exec** REPLAY
     }
not FI [*Increaser*$4 ->] **break** *Increaser*| (2)
     [*Increaser*$6!T ->] {   (3)
     FI := FALSE; **exec** REPLAY
     }
not FD [*Decreaser*$4 ->] **break** *Decreaser*| (4)
     [*Decreaser*$8!T ->] {   (5)
     FD := FALSE; **exec** REPLAY
     }
not FC [*Consumer*$3 ->] **break** *Consumer*| (6)
     [*Consumer*$6!T ->] {   (7)
     FC := FALSE; **exec** REPLAY
     }

The Boolean registers FI, FD and FC implement the process flags,
and the character register PID contains a process identifier. Upon
the beginning of the execution of the program, directive (1) executes
the command script REPLAY, which is as follows:

```
script REPLAY {
    rget PID from TRACE
    switch
        case PID = 'I' :
            FI := TRUE; run Increaser|
        case PID = 'D' :
            FD := TRUE; run Decreaser|
        case PID = 'C' :
            FC := TRUE; run Consumer|
    end switch
}
```

The first command of this script reads the next process identifier from the file TRACE into the register PID. The second command sets the flag associated with the process identified by the contents of PID, and switches this process into run state.

On the beginning of the execution of the statement :*Sharing:Increaser*$4 (a *P* operation), if the flag associated with the process *Increaser* is cleared, directive (2) switches this process into break state. On termination of the execution of the statement :*Sharing:Increaser*$6 (a *V* operation), directive (3) clears the flag associated with *Increaser*, and executes REPLAY. Similar actions are performed by directives (4) and (5) for the process *Decreaser*, and by directives (6) and (7) for the process *Consumer*.

7.9 DETECTING TIMING ERRORS

A *timing error*, also called a *race condition* [Krishnamurthy, 1989], is a situation in which process interactions take place in an order different from that which is expected [Garcia-Molina, 1984]. For instance, consider a reading and a writing process sharing access to a given variable. If the programmer intends the reading process to read the value written by the writing process, he must ensure that the two operations always take place in the order (write, read). If he fails to do so, the actual order of the operations will depend on several factors, such as the processor load and process scheduling, which vary between executions. It is often necessary to run the program many times to expose the error.

Problem 7.8

Let us consider again the erroneous implementation of the process *Decreaser* of the program *Sharing*, shown in Figure 7.3. If *Decreaser* always acquires exclusive access to the variable *shared* immediately after execution of the statement :*Sharing*:*Decreaser*$4, the program behaves as expected. However, the error will become evident if we run the program several times with different process scheduling orders. The directives which follow force the processes *Increaser*, *Decreaser* and *Consumer* to acquire exclusive access to *shared*, in turn:

$$
\begin{array}{lll}
& \textbf{allocate}\ \text{IR, DR, CR : BOOLEAN} & \\
\text{IR} & [\ Increaser\$4 \rightarrow]\ \textbf{break}\ Increaser| & (1) \\
& [\ Increaser\$6!T \rightarrow]\ \{ & (2) \\
& \quad \text{IR := TRUE; DR := TRUE} & \\
& \quad \textbf{run}\ Decreaser| & \\
& \quad \} & \\
\textbf{not}\ \text{DR} & [\ Decreaser\$6, Decreaser\$10 \rightarrow]\ \backslash & (3) \\
& \quad \textbf{break}\ Decreaser| & \\
& [\ Decreaser\$8!T, Decreaser\$12!T \rightarrow]\ \{ & (4) \\
& \quad \text{DR := FALSE; CR := TRUE} & \\
& \quad \textbf{run}\ Consumer| & \\
& \quad \} & \\
\textbf{not}\ \text{CR} & [\ Consumer\$3 \rightarrow]\ \textbf{break}\ Consumer| & (5) \\
& [\ Consumer\$6!T \rightarrow]\ \{ & (6) \\
& \quad \text{CR := FALSE; IR := FALSE} & \\
& \quad \textbf{run}\ Increaser| & \\
& \quad \} & \\
\end{array}
$$

The Boolean registers IR, DR and CR are associated with *Increaser*, *Decreaser* and *Consumer*, respectively. *Increaser* is allowed to execute a *P* operation on the semaphore *mutex* only if IR is cleared. If this is not the case, directive (1) switches the process into break state. When *Increaser* terminates execution of a *V* operation, directive (2) sets IR and DR, and switches *Decreaser* into run state. In this way, only *Decreaser* will be allowed to enter the critical section. Similar effects are produced by directives (3) and (4) for the process *Decreaser*, and by directives (5) and (6) for the process *Consumer*, respectively. On the beginning of the execution of the program, the register IR is cleared, thus allowing *Increaser* to be the first process to enter the critical section.

Chapter 8

The debugging of message-passing concurrent programs

Objective

This chapter considers the concurrent programming languages which use message passing for interprocess communication and synchronization. The language constructs for message exchange are presented. Examples of debugging experiments are then proposed, which show the utilization of the PDE command language in debugging message-passing concurrent programs.

Contents

8.1   INTRODUCTION

In a message-passing concurrent program, the component processes operate within disjoint logical address spaces. Interprocess interactions take place by means of explicit message exchanges. A pair of message-passing operations, which we will call *send* and *receive*, make it possible to establish a logical connection, called a *communication link*, between two processes. Synchronization between the communicating processes comes from precedence constraint between message sending and receipt.

8.1.1   Communication

Message-passing statements can be classified according to the mechanisms used *(a)* to name the source and the destination process of a communication link, and *(b)* to synchronize the communicating processes. From the point of view of process naming, interprocess communication can be classified into direct symmetric, direct asymmetric or indirect communication [Silberschatz, 1991]. In *direct symmetric* communication, each process explicitly names the other as the destination or the source in a *send* or a *receive* operation. In this form of communication, these operations are expressed as

  send (message, destination)

and

  receive (message, source)

In *direct asymmetric* communication, only the sender specifies the intended receiver; whereas the receiver obtains the name of the sender as an output parameter of the *receive* operation. This parameter, which we will identify as *process_id*, is of the language-defined type *process*. The *receive* operation is now as follows:

  process_id := receive (message)

Finally, in *indirect communication*, processes communicate via mailboxes. A *mailbox* is a recipient into which messages can be inserted and from which messages can be extracted. In its simplest form, a mailbox is just a global object whose name can appear as the destination or the source in the *send* and *receive* operations. The communication primitives are now

> *send* (*message, mailbox*)

and

> *process_id* := *receive* (*message, mailbox*)

These operations allow a process to send a message to, and receive a message from, the named mailbox. A process which receives a message also obtains the name of the message sender in the output parameter *process_id* of the *receive* operation.

Direct naming is well suited for expressing pipelining. A *pipeline* is a sequence of two or more concurrent processes such that each process receives its input from the preceding one and sends its output to the following one. On the other hand, indirect naming and mailboxes allow a straightforward implementation of *client/server* interactions. In a client/server relationship, a server process provides service to a number of client processes. A client requests a service by sending a message to the server. The server receives a request message, accomplishes the service and, if necessary, sends a reply message to the client, cyclically. The client/server relationship can be many-to-one or many-to-many. In the latter case, more than one server can name the same mailbox.

A *port* is a mailbox which holds messages of a specific type. Each port has a single receiver, i.e. the process which created that port. A port declaration has the form of a variable declaration, as follows:

> **port** <port identifier> : <message type>

Port identifiers are exported from the declaring process to the external environment, so that they may be used by other processes as a parameter in *send* operations. The dot notation makes it possible to discriminate between ports with the same name declared within different processes, as follows:

> <process identifier>.<port identifier>

Ports are especially well suited for implementing servers which provide several services. A server of this type features one port for each service. To request a specific service, a client inserts a message into the port corresponding to this service.

8.1.2 Synchronization

From the point of view of synchronization, interprocess communication can be classified into synchronous, buffered or asynchronous communication [Andrews, 1983]. In a *synchronous* communication, the first of the two communicating processes which executes a *send* or *receive* operation must wait for the other process to arrive at the communication point. The information transfer involved in the message transmission can now take place. In a *buffered* communication, a buffer with a bounded capacity is associated with the communication link; when the buffer becomes full, the sender must wait until space becomes available. Finally, in an *asynchronous* communication, the execution of a *send* operation does not delay the sender, whose execution can always proceed immediately after the message has been delivered. The message system is responsible for implementing the required form of unlimited message buffering.

Usually, a process which executes a *receive* operation blocks until a message is available on the communication link. However, a number of languages provide a form of nonblocking *receive*. In this case, the operation tests whether a message is available on the communication link and, if it is not, returns a negative indication. For instance, a nonblocking *receive* allows a process to select a communication link with at least one message available. However, if a process needs a message from a specific link and no message is available on that link, the process must perform repeated tests by iteratively executing the *receive* operation: this is a form of busy waiting.

8.1.3 Guarded statements

Busy waiting can be avoided by using *guarded statements* [Dijkstra, 1975].* A statement of this type consists of a *statement guard* and a

---

* We use the terms *guarded statement* and *statement guard* instead of, respectively, the more common *guarded command* and *guard*, to avoid possible confusion with the PDE commands, and the command guards in guarded directives.

statement sequence. The symbol '->' separates the statement guard
and the statement sequence as follows:

    <statement guard> -> <statement sequence>

The statement guard consists of a Boolean expression and a synchronous message-passing operation separated by the symbol ';' as
follows:

    <Boolean expression> ; <message-passing operation>

Both the message-passing operation and the Boolean expression are
optional. A statement guard with no Boolean expression specification is equivalent to a statement guard whose Boolean expression is
always true. A guard *fails* if the evaluation of the Boolean expression produces the value *false*, or the process named in the message-
passing operation is terminated. A non-failing guard *succeeds* if it
does not specify a message-passing operation, or if this operation
can be executed immediately. A *delayed* guard is a non-failing, non-
succeeding guard. The execution of a guarded statement evaluates
the guard. If the guard fails, the process which contains the guarded
statement terminates abnormally, otherwise the message-passing
operation (if present) is completed and the statement sequence is
then executed.

    Guarded statements may be used within non-deterministic alter-
native and iterative statements. In a possible notation, a non-deterministic alternative statement consists of a sequence of guarded
statements separated by the keyword **or** and bracketed by the delimiters **alt** and **end alt**, as follows:

```
alt
   <guarded statement>
or
   <guarded statement>
or
   ...
or
   <guarded statement>
end alt
```

The execution evaluates the guards of the component statements. If all the guards fail, the alternative statement fails, and the process containing this statement terminates abnormally. If at least one guard succeeds, one of them is selected non-deterministically, i.e. the language does not define which one. If all the non-failing guards are delayed, the process containing the alternative statement is suspended until a guard succeeds.

An iterative statement consists of a sequence of guarded statements separated by the keyword **or** and bracketed by the delimiters **do** and **end do**, as follows:

```
do
   <guarded statement>
or
   <guarded statement>
or
   ...
or
   <guarded statement>
end do
```

The actions involved in each iteration are similar to those involved in the execution of an alternative statement. However, if all the guards fail, the execution of the iterative statement is successfully completed.

8.1.4   Remote procedure calls

The specification of client/server interactions is facilitated by the *remote procedure call* programming language construct. Unlike a local procedure, a remote procedure is executed in a different process, possibly on a separate computer. Therefore, a remote procedure call and its parameters are exchanged between the client and the server in the form of messages.

In a possible notation, a remote procedure takes the form of an **accept** statement, which specifies both the receipt of a request for a service and the execution of the service. This statement is as follows:

accept <remote procedure identifier> (<formal parameter list>)
do <statement sequence> **end**

The statement sequence specifies the actions to be performed in response to the request. A server process will feature at least one remote procedure for each different service. To request a given service, a client calls the remote procedure which corresponds to that
service by means of the **call** statement, which has the form

call <server identifier>.<remote procedure identifier> (<actual
parameter list>)

The dot notation is used to specify a given remote procedure of the
named server. Each actual parameter must have the same type as the
corresponding formal parameter in the **accept** statement. A parameter can be an input parameter or an output parameter. An actual input
parameter must be an expression, and an actual output parameter
must be a variable. The server may even contain more than one **accept** statement for the same remote procedure. All these statements
will feature the same remote procedure identifier. In this way, the
server may perform different actions in response to a given request
for a service, depending, for instance, on the state of the resources
it manages.

Communication between a client and the server occurs via a call
and the acceptance of the call. The transfer of information between
the two processes occurs via the input and the output parameters of
the call, before starting up and after terminating the execution of the
statement sequence specified by the **accept** statement. Communication is synchronous; a remote procedure call blocks the client until
the server has terminated the execution of the procedure. It follows
that a remote procedure call is equivalent to a synchronous *send*
immediately followed by a blocking *receive*.

The following sections present a number of message-passing
concurrent programs in which the different language constructs are
used to implement various forms of process interaction. We will illustrate a number of significant debugging problems and solutions
by using the PDE command language.

8.2 TRACING MESSAGE-PASSING ACTIVITIES

When debugging a message-passing program, the programmer is often involved in monitoring message-passing activities. As the following problems illustrate, the result of the monitoring can be obtained by using a form of selective tracing.

Problem 8.1

The program *Buffering* shown in Figure 8.1 is written in a message-passing concurrent language which features synchronous message passing and direct, symmetric communication. The program consists of four processes, called *BB*, *Producer1*, *Producer2* and *Consumer*. *BB* implements a bounded buffer which can store up to *n* items. These items are sent by *Producer1* and *Producer2* for utilization by *Consumer*. *BB* keeps the items in the array *buffer*, which is treated as a circular array, with the last array element considered adjacent to the first. The variables *in* and *out* contain the index of the next free and the last used array element, and the variable *count* indicates the number of items available in the buffer.

The body of *BB* consists of a variable initialization section and a non-deterministic iterative statement. The variables *in* and *out* are both initialized to 1, and *count* is initialized to 0 to indicate that the buffer is empty at the outset. In the iterative statement, the guards guarantee that items are neither extracted from the buffer when it is empty, nor added to the buffer when it is full. The insertions and extractions take place in a non-deterministic order. When free space is available in the buffer (which is indicated by any value of *count* less than *n*), *BB* can receive a message from *Producer1* or *Producer2* by means of the receive statements *BB*$6 and *BB*$9, respectively. When items are available in the buffer (which is indicated by any value of *count* greater than 0), *BB* can send a message to *Consumer* by means of the send statement *BB*$12. Following the receipt or the sending of a message, *BB* updates *count* as well as *in* or *out* to reflect the change in the buffer state.

With reference to the program *Buffering*, we want to trace: *(a)* the contents of the messages sent by *BB* to *Consumer*; and *(b)* the path followed by the control flow of the process *BB* at the level of the execution of the *send* and *receive* operations.

```
          {:Buffering}    program Buffering;
     {:Buffering:item}      type item = ...;
       {:Buffering:BB}      process BB; {bounded buffer}
     {:Buffering:BB:n}        const n = ...;
{:Buffering:BB:buffer}        var buffer : array [1..n] of item;
    {:Buffering:BB:in}          in,
   {:Buffering:BB:out}          out : 1..n;
 {:Buffering:BB:count}          count : 0..n;
     {:Buffering:BB$1}      begin {BB}
                  {$2}        in := 1;
                  {$3}        out := 1;
                  {$4}        count := 0;
                  {$5}        do   count < n;
                  {$6}             receive (buffer [in], Producer1) ->
                  {$7}                in := in mod n + 1;
                  {$8}                count := count + 1
                             or   count < n;
                  {$9}             receive (buffer [in], Producer2) ->
                 {$10}                in := in mod n + 1;
                 {$11}                count := count + 1
                             or   count > 0;
                 {$12}             send (buffer [out], Consumer) ->
                 {$13}                out := out mod n + 1;
                 {$14}                count := count - 1
                             end  do
                           end; {BB}
  {:Buffering:Producer1}    process Producer1;
{:Buffering:Producer1:m}      var m : item;
{:Buffering:Producer1$1}    begin {Producer1}
                  {$2}        repeat
                  {$3}          ...;  {produce an item in m}
                  {$4}          send (m, BB)
                             until false
                           end; {Producer1}
  {:Buffering:Producer2}    process Producer2;
{:Buffering:Producer2:m}      var m : item;
{:Buffering:Producer2$1}    begin {Producer2}
                  {$2}        repeat
                  {$3}          ...;  {produce an item in m}
                  {$4}          send (m, BB)
                             until false
                           end; {Producer2}
```

Figure 8.1 Concurrent program *Buffering*.

```
{:Buffering:Consumer}          process Consumer;
{:Buffering:Consumer:m}           var m : item;
{:Buffering:Consumer$1}        begin {Consumer}
              {$2}                repeat
              {$3}                  receive (m, BB);
              {$...}                  ...   {consume the item m}
                                  until false
                                end {Consumer}
                              end. {Buffering}
```

Figure 8.1 *Continued.*

Solution: *(a)*

[*BB*$12!T ->] **put** *BB:buffer* [*BB:out*]   (1)

On termination of every execution of the send statement *BB*$12, the **put** command in this directive displays the value of the item sent by *BB* to *Consumer*.

(b)

[*BB*$6!T ->] **put** 'Receive from Producer1'   (1)
[*BB*$9!T ->] **put** 'Receive from Producer2'   (2)
[*BB*$12!T ->] **put** 'Send to Consumer'   (3)

Each time *BB* receives a message from either producer, the **put** commands in directives (1) and (2) display an appropriate message on the console. A similar action is performed by directive (3) each time *BB* sends a message to *Consumer*.

Problem 8.2

The program *Wakeup* given in Figure 8.2 is written in a concurrent language using ports for synchronous, indirect interprocess communication. This program consists of a server process *AC* (an alarm clock) and a number of client processes *Client1*, ..., *ClientM*. The server supplies the clients with a wake-up service, which consists of suspending the execution of a requesting client until a given number of occasions has occurred.

```
              {:Wakeup}         program Wakeup;
        {:Wakeup:nonegint}        type nonegint = 0..maxint;

             {:Wakeup:AC}         process AC; {alarm clock}
     {:Wakeup:AC:newoccp}          port newoccp : signal;
     {:Wakeup:AC:setalarmp}         setalarmp : nonegint;
     {:Wakeup:AC:totalocc}        var totalocc : nonegint;
        {:Wakeup:AC:pid}            pid,
      {:Wakeup:AC:client}           client : process;
       {:Wakeup:AC:wnum}            wnum : nonegint;
     {:Wakeup:AC:wakeupq}           wakeupq : ...; {queue of
                                                wake-up requests}
      {:Wakeup:AC:newocc}          newocc,
    {:Wakeup:AC:wakeupsig}         wakeupsig : signal;
      {:Wakeup:AC:Insert}        procedure Insert (
  {:Wakeup:AC:Insert:client}        client : process;
   {:Wakeup:AC:Insert:wnum}         wnum : nonegint);
     {:Wakeup:AC:Insert$1}       begin {Insert}
               {$...}             ...   {insert a wake-up
                                        request into wakeupq}
                                 end; {Insert}
     {:Wakeup:AC:Extract}        function Extract (
 {:Wakeup:AC:Extract:client}       var client : process
 {:Wakeup:AC:Extract:Extract}      ) : boolean;
   {:Wakeup:AC:Extract$1}        begin {Extract}
               {$...}             ...   {extract a wake-up
                                        request from wakeupq}
                                 end; {Extract}
       {:Wakeup:AC$1}            begin {AC}
               {$2}               totalocc := 0;
               {$3}               do
               {$4}                 pid := receive (newocc,
                                      newoccp) ->
               {$5}                   totalocc := totalocc + 1;
               {$6}                   while Extract (client)
               {$7}                   do send (wakeupsig, client)
                                    or
               {$8}                 client := receive (wnum,
                                      setalarmp) ->
               {$9}                   wnum := wnum + totalocc;
               {$10}                  Insert (client, wnum)
                                 end do
                                 end; {AC}
```

Figure 8.2 Concurrent program *Wakeup*.

```
        {:Wakeup:Observer}              process Observer;
  {:Wakeup:Observer:newocc}               var newocc : signal;
    {:Wakeup:Observer$1}               begin {Observer}
                   {$2}                  repeat
                   {$3}                    ...;  {detect the occurrence of an
                                                  occasion}
                   {$4}                    send (newocc, AC.newoccp)
                                         until false
                                       end; {Observer}


       {:Wakeup:Client1}               process Client1;
  {:Wakeup:Client1:wnum}                 var wnum : nonegint;
 {:Wakeup:Client1:wakeupsig}                 wakeupsig : signal;
    {:Wakeup:Client1$1}                begin {Client1}
                   {$2}                  repeat
                   {$3}                    ...;
                   {$4}                    send (wnum, AC.setalarmp);
                   {$5}                    receive (wakeupsig, AC);
                 {$...}                    ...
                                         until false
                                       end; {Client1}
                                       ...;
       {:Wakeup:ClientM}               process ClientM;
  {:Wakeup:ClientM:wnum}                 var wnum : nonegint;
 {:Wakeup:ClientM:wakeupsig}                 wakeupsig : signal;
    {:Wakeup:ClientM$1}                begin {ClientM}
                   {$2}                  repeat
                   {$3}                    ...;
                   {$4}                    send (wnum, AC.setalarmp);
                   {$5}                    receive (wakeupsig, AC);
                 {$...}                    ...
                                         until false
                                       end {ClientM}

                                       end. {Wakeup}
```

Figure 8.2 *Continued.*

AC uses the local variable *totalocc* to keep track of the total number of occasions. *AC* increases the value of *totalocc* by one each time it receives a message of the *signal* type from the process *Observer* via the port *newoccp*. The *signal* message type is defined by the language, and corresponds to empty messages used for synchronization purposes. *Observer* inserts a signal into *newoccp* each time it detects a new occasion.

If a client wishes to be suspended it sends a service request message to the port *setalarmp* of *AC*, and then executes a *receive* operation in order to wait for a wake-up signal from *AC*. The service request message specifies the duration of the suspension, which is expressed in terms of the number *wnum* of new occasions to be detected before being woken up. On receiving this message, *AC* adds *wnum* to the total number of occasions (contained in *totalocc*) to obtain the client's wake-up occasion number. *AC* then executes the *Insert* procedure to insert this number together with the client's identifier into a queue of wake-up requests, called *wakeupq*. On each new occasion, *AC* executes the function *Extract* to inspect the queue and obtain the identifiers of the clients to be woken up. A signal is sent to each of these clients. *Extract* searches *wakeupq* for a wake-up request scheduled for the present occasion number (contained in *totalocc*). If the search is successful, this function extracts the request from the queue and returns the Boolean value *true* and the client's identifier; otherwise, *Extract* returns *false*.

With reference to the program *Wakeup*, we want to trace the program activity at the level of: *(a)* the non-deterministic choices performed by the process *AC* in the execution of the iterative statement *AC*$3; *(b)* the messages exchanged between *AC* and the client processes; and *(c)* the operations performed on *wakeupq*.

Solution: *(a)*

> [*AC*$4!T ->] **put** 'New occasion'   (1)
> [*AC*$8!T ->] **put** 'Service request: ', *AC:client*, \   (2)
>   *AC:wnum*

Directive (1) displays a message on the console each time *AC* receives a signal from *Observer*. A similar action is performed by directive (2) each time *AC* receives a service request from a client. In this case, the message includes the client's identifier and the duration of the suspension.

(b)

$$[AC\$7!T ->] \textbf{ put } \text{'Wake up: ', } AC:client \qquad (1)$$
$$[AC\$8!T ->] \textbf{ put } \text{'Wait: ', } AC:client, AC:wnum \qquad (2)$$

Each time *AC* sends a wake-up signal to a client, the **put** command in directive (1) displays the client's identifier. A similar action is performed by directive (2) each time *AC* receives a service request from a client.

(c)

$$[\textit{Extract}\$1!T ->] \textbf{ put } \text{'Request extracted'} \qquad (1)$$
$$[\textit{Insert}\$1!T ->] \textbf{ put } \text{'Request inserted'} \qquad (2)$$

Directive (1) displays a message on the console each time *AC* extracts a wake-up request from *wakeupq*. A similar action is performed by directive (2) each time *AC* inserts a wake-up request into *wakeupq*.

8.3 CONDITIONAL BREAK TRAPS

In this section we will show applications of conditional break traps in monitoring a message-passing program at the level of significant process interactions.

Problem 8.3

With reference to the program *Wakeup*, we want to generate a break trap to the processes *AC* and *Observer*: *(a)* whenever a client resumes execution; *(b)* each time that all the clients have sent at least one message to *AC*; and *(c)* whenever all the clients are suspended and waiting for a wake-up signal.

Solution: *(a)*

$$[AC\$7!T ->] \textbf{ break } AC|, \textit{Observer}| \qquad (1)$$

For the sake of clarity, we will show the solutions to cases *(b)* and *(c)* in the hypothesis of two clients (the extension to more clients can be easily imagined).

(b)

allocate C1, C2 : BOOLEAN
not C1 [*Client1*$4!T ->] C1 := TRUE   (1)
not C2 [*Client2*$4!T ->] C2 := TRUE   (2)
C1 **and** C2 [->] {   (3)
      C1 := FALSE; C2 := FALSE
      break *AC*|, *Observer*|
      }

Directive (1) sets the Boolean register C1 the first time *Client1* sends a message to *AC*. A similar action is performed by directive (2) with respect to *Client2* and the Boolean register C2. When both C1 and C2 are set, directive (3) clears these two registers and then generates the desired break trap.

(c)

allocate COUNT : BOOLEAN
  [*Insert*$1!T ->] COUNT := COUNT + 1   (1)
  [*Extract*$1!T ->] COUNT := COUNT - 1   (2)
COUNT = 2 [->] {   (3)
      COUNT := 0
      break *AC*|, *Observer*|
      }

The integer register COUNT is used to count the number of wake-up requests in *wakeupq*. Directives (1) and (2) increase and decrease the value of this register by one whenever *AC* inserts or extracts a wake-up request from the queue. When the value of COUNT is two, directive (3) clears COUNT and generates the desired break trap.

Problem 8.4

With reference to the program *Buffering*, we want to generate a break trap to the process *BB* whenever the buffer becomes full.

Solution:

[*BB*:count!W -> *BB*:count = *BB*:n] **break** *BB*| (1)

8.4 STEPWISE EXECUTION

As seen in Section 6.7, stepwise execution periodically generates traps. In message-passing concurrent programs, the trap generation period can, for example, be expressed in terms of the number of messages exchanged. Problem 8.5 shows an application of this technique in the generation of break traps.

Problem 8.5

The program *RemoteBuffering* shown in Figure 8.3 is written in a concurrent language which uses remote procedure calls. The program defines a process, called *RB*, which encapsulates a buffer with a capacity of a single item. This buffer can be accessed by means of two remote procedures, called *put* and *get*, which make it possible to deposit an item in the buffer and to extract an item from the buffer. *RB* accepts the calls to *put* and *get* in the order given, thereby preventing an item from being extracted when the buffer is empty, and from being inserted when the buffer is full. *RB* is a server process: the clients are the producer processes *Producer1* and *Producer2*, and the consumer process *Consumer*.

In the program *RemoteBuffering*, the following directives generate a break trap to *Producer1* whenever this process has sent a given number of messages to the process *RB*:

```
        allocate PERIOD, COUNT : INTEGER
        [ Producer1$1 -> ] rget PERIOD
        [ Producer1$4!T -> ] COUNT := COUNT + 1      (1)
   COUNT = PERIOD [ -> ] {                           (2)
        COUNT := 0
        break Producer1|
        }
```

The register PERIOD is meant to contain the trap generation period, expressed in terms of the number of messages sent by *Producer1* to *RB*. The register COUNT counts these messages. As soon as the execution of *Producer1* begins, the trap generation period is read from the console and stored in PERIOD. Directive (1) increases COUNT by one whenever *Producer1* sends a message to *RB*. If the

```
        {:RemoteBuffering}          program RemoteBuffering;
      {:RemoteBuffering:item}         type item = ...;

      {:RemoteBuffering:RB}          process RB; {remote buffer}
      {:RemoteBuffering:RB:i}          var i : item;
      {:RemoteBuffering:RB$1}         begin {RB}
               {$2}                      repeat
               {$3}                        accept put (in m : item)
               {$4}                          do i := m
                                            end;
               {$5}                        accept get (out m : item)
               {$6}                          do m := i
                                            end
                                          until false
                                        end; {RB}

    {:RemoteBuffering:Producer1}      process Producer1;
   {:RemoteBuffering:Producer1:m}       var m : item;
   {:RemoteBuffering:Producer1$1}      begin {Producer1}
               {$2}                      repeat
               {$3}                        ...; {produce an item in m}
               {$4}                        call RB.put (m)
                                          until false
                                        end; {Producer1}

    {:RemoteBuffering:Producer2}      process Producer2;
   {:RemoteBuffering:Producer2:m}       var m : item;
   {:RemoteBuffering:Producer2$1}      begin {Producer2}
               {$2}                      repeat
               {$3}                        ...; {produce an item in m}
               {$4}                        call RB.put (m)
                                          until false
                                        end; {Producer2}

    {:RemoteBuffering:Consumer}       process Consumer;
   {:RemoteBuffering:Consumer:m}        var m : item;
   {:RemoteBuffering:Consumer$1}       begin {Consumer}
               {$2}                      repeat
               {$3}                        call RB.get (m);
               {$...}                       ... {consume the item m}
                                          until false
                                        end {Consumer}

                                    end. {RemoteBuffering}
```

Figure 8.3 Concurrent program *RemoteBuffering*.

new value of COUNT is equal to the trap generation period, directive (2) clears COUNT and generates the desired break trap.

8.5 DETECTING DEADLOCK SITUATIONS

As seen in Section 7.7, deadlock situations may be caused by programming errors. The following problem deals with detecting such a situation.

Problem 8.6

The program *Alternate*, shown in Figure 8.4, is written in a concurrent language which features synchronous message passing and direct, symmetric communication. The program defines two processes P and Q which alternate in the roles of producer and consumer. The two processes have a similar structure. In each of them, the local variable r indicates the role (producer or consumer). Initially, P is the producer. It generates an item, and sends this item to Q. When the message has been delivered, the roles are switched.

The behaviour of the processes which form *Alternate* depends on the correct specification of the values of the variables $P{:}r$ and $Q{:}r$. For instance, if $P{:}r$ is erroneously initialized to *consumer*, a deadlock situation occurs from the first iteration of the non-deterministic statements $P\$3$ and $Q\$3$, since each process will be suspended while waiting for a message from the other. The following directives detect situations of this type:

> **allocate** PMSG, QMSG : BOOLEAN
> [$P\$5, P\$7 ->$] PMSG := TRUE (1)
> [$P\$5!T, P\$7!T ->$] PMSG := FALSE (2)
> [$Q\$5, Q\$7 ->$] QMSG := TRUE (3)
> [$Q\$5!T, Q\$7!T ->$] QMSG := FALSE (4)
> PMSG **and** QMSG [$-> P{:}r = Q{:}r$] \ (5)
> **rput** 'Deadlock detected'

Directives (1) and (2) set and clear the Boolean register PMSG each time the process P begins and terminates the execution of a message-passing operation, respectively. Similar actions are carried out

```
        {:Alternate}    program Alternate;
     {:Alternate:item}     type item = ...;
     {:Alternate:role}       role = (producer, consumer);

       {:Alternate:P}     process P;
      {:Alternate:P:r}       var r : role;
      {:Alternate:P:m}         m : item;
     {:Alternate:P$1}     begin {P}
             {$2}           r := producer;
             {$3}           do r = producer ->
             {$4}                 ...; {produce an item in m}
             {$5}                 send (m, Q);
             {$6}                 r := consumer
                            or r = consumer ->
             {$7}                 receive (m, Q);
             {$8}                 ...; {consume the item m}
             {$9}                 r := producer
                            end do
                          end; {P}

       {:Alternate:Q}     process Q;
      {:Alternate:Q:r}       var r : role;
      {:Alternate:Q:m}         m : item;
     {:Alternate:Q$1}     begin {Q}
             {$2}           r := consumer;
             {$3}           do r = producer ->
             {$4}                 ...; {produce an item in m}
             {$5}                 send (m, P);
             {$6}                 r := consumer
                            or r = consumer ->
             {$7}                 receive (m, P);
             {$8}                 ...; {consume the item m}
             {$9}                 r := producer
                            end do
                          end; {Q}

                      end. {Alternate}
```

Figure 8.4 Concurrent program *Alternate*.

by directives (3) and (4) for the process *Q* and the Boolean register QMSG. When both PMSG and QMSG are set, if the value of *P:r* is equal to that of *Q:r*, a deadlock situation has occurred, and directive (5) generates a warning message.

8.6 CONTROLLING NON-DETERMINISTIC SELECTIONS

When writing a message-passing program with forms of non-deterministic selection, the programmer should not hypothesize any specific selection criteria, since the selection algorithm is in fact implementation-dependent. On the other hand, in the program-debugging phase, the programmer may want to exert control over non-deterministic selections in order, for instance, to detect an error which may have been masked by a specific choice. In a different application, forcing specific selection criteria can be useful to isolate the different aspects of the program behaviour and to analyse each of them separately. The following problem shows an example.

Problem 8.7

With reference to the program *Buffering*, we want to avoid overflow situations in which all the elements of the buffer are full.

Solution:

$$[BB\$6, BB\$9 -> BB:count = (BB:n - 1)] \backslash \qquad (1)$$
$$BB|@ := BB\$12$$

At the beginning of the execution of either receive statement $BB\$6$ or $BB\$9$, if the value of the variable *count* is equal to $BB:n - 1$, directive (1) modifies the value of the current statement pointer $BB|@$ of the process BB and forces BB to execute the send statement $BB\$12$.

8.7 REPLAYING PROGRAM EXECUTION

As seen in Section 7.3, a cyclical concurrent-program debugging experiment consists of a monitoring phase and one or more replay phases. In the monitoring phase, we collect the sequence of the process interactions and the data values associated with these interactions in a replay trace. This trace will be used in the replay phases to drive the non-deterministic aspects of program execution.

In a message-passing concurrent program, the replay trace includes the results of the non-deterministic choices and the contents of the messages exchanged between the concurrent processes.

Problem 8.8

With reference to the program *Buffering*, we want to replay the execution of the process *BB*.

Solution:

In the monitoring phase of this experiment, we activate the following directives:

[*BB*$6!T, *BB*$9!T, *BB*$12!T ->] **rput** *BB*|@ \   (1)
   append to STMTFILE

[*BB*$6!T, *BB*$9!T ->] **put** *BB*:*buffer* [*BB*:*in*] \   (2)
   append to MSGFILE

These directives gather the program replay trace in the STMTFILE and MSGFILE files, which contain the results of the non-deterministic choices and the message contents, respectively. On termination of the execution of any of the message-passing statements *BB*$6, *BB*$9 and *BB*$12, directive (1) records the alternative chosen in the non-deterministic statement *BB*$5 by appending the value of the current statement pointer *BB*|@ of the process *BB* to STMTFILE. Directive (2) records the contents of the message received by *BB* by appending these contents to the file MSGFILE on termination of the execution of either receive statement *BB*$6 or *BB*$9.

In the replay phase, before starting up a new execution of the program, we activate the following directives:

[*BB*$6, *BB*$9, *BB*$12 ->] \   (1)
   rget *BB*|@ **from** STMTFILE

[*BB*$6!T, *BB*$9!T ->] **get** *BB*:*buffer* [*BB*:*in*] \   (2)
   from MSGFILE

At the beginning of each iteration of the non-deterministic statement *BB*$5, directive (1) forces the current statement pointer *BB*|@ to contain the same value as in the monitoring phase by taking this value from STMTFILE. In this way, the sequence of message-passing statements executed by *BB* will be reproduced. Moreover, if either receive statement *BB*$6 or *BB*$9 is selected, directive (2) causes *BB* to receive the same message as in the monitoring phase, by substituting the contents of the buffer element involved in the receive statement with quantities taken from MSGFILE.

Chapter 9

Measuring program performance

Objective

This chapter shows applications of the PDE command language to answer a number of questions about program resource demands. The problem of performance evaluation is approached from the point of view of the performance both of the program source code, and of the object code generated by the compiler. Examples of dynamic measurement of program behaviour are presented. They are aimed at identifying the program portions responsible for high resource consumption. Experiments on program structure analysis are illustrated. The results can profitably be used to design the compiler and the processor architecture.

Contents

9.1 INTRODUCTION

Many programs have performance objectives. Program performance is evaluated to improve program behaviour in terms of resource demands. This problem can be dealt with on two levels: that of the program source code and that of the object code, which is generated by the compiler.

9.1.1 Performance bugs

The performance of the source code can be improved by eliminating the so-called *performance bugs* [Ferrari, 1978], i.e. by identifying the program portions which are responsible for high resource utilization, in terms of both the processor time needed to perform the computation and the memory space required to store the data objects generated by the computation.

Profiling is a technique aimed at identifying performance bugs. An *execution profile* contains the number of times the different program fragments have been executed in a given program run. The profile can be at the statement, block or subprogram level [Ponder, 1988]. By multiplying the frequency of execution of a given fragment by the number of memory accesses generated by the machine instructions which translate that fragment, we obtain the total memory access cost of the fragment. We can use the results of the profiling activities to enhance the algorithms used in the critical program portions, i.e. those portions which are responsible for most of the execution times.

Data representation and the number of subprogram activations are important factors in memory space. This is particularly the case with recursive subprograms. In these subprograms, the memory requirements for the local variables must be multiplied by the number of recursive activations generated by the given subprogram run to obtain an evaluation of the memory space demands for that run.

9.1.2 Program structure analysis

Efficient implementation of a block-structured high-level language requires an in-depth analysis of the static structure and the dynamic behaviour of typical computations. The statistics which can be gathered on these program aspects are mainly concerned with the accesses to the program variables, and the subprogram calls. The results of this analysis are useful in the design of the compiler and in the development of the processor architecture, particularly in the memory addressing mechanisms.

It has been demonstrated that subprogram calls and returns are responsible for a high fraction of the program execution times [Katevenis, 1985], [Lazzerini, 1989a], [Patterson, 1982]. This is a consequence of the high number of subprogram calls, and the high execution time cost of the machine instructions which translate a call. The efficiency of the subprogram invocation mechanisms tends to affect strongly program performance.

As seen in Chapter 2, the scope rules of a block-structured language, which are based on the static nesting of block declarations, state that an entity local to a given block is visible in this block and in all blocks statically nested within this block. An exception is an entity whose identifier has been reused to name a different entity in a block at a higher static lexical level; in this case, the former entity will be masked out by the latter.

With reference to the program tree representation, we have defined the static lexical level of a given program block as the distance between this block and the root of the tree. The variable accesses can be classified according to the position of the variable declaration in the tree. An access performed by a statement declared in a given block is *local* if the variable is declared in the same block, *global* if the variable is declared in the outermost block, and *intermediate* if it is neither local nor global [De Prycker, 1982a].

The execution of a block-structured program creates a stack of *activation records* [Ghezzi, 1987]. When a new instance of a program block is generated, e.g. when a block statement or subprogram is entered, a new activation record is created and pushed onto the stack. This record contains all the information needed to execute that block, including the locations reserved for storage of the values of the local variables, and two pointers called the *static link* and the *dynamic link*. The static link of the activation record of any given block B points to the activation record of the block that statically encloses B. The dynamic link points to the activation record of the block which activated B. It follows that the dynamic link chain which originates from the activation record of the current block identifies the sequence of the block instances which are dynamically generated by the program execution.

Within a block, each local variable is statically bound to the offset of the memory location reserved for that variable in the activation record of that block. At run time, a local reference is solved simply by using the offset; a non-local reference requires searching each activation record in the chain of the static links which originates from the activation record of the current block until an identifier match is found. Alternatively, the compiler evaluates the difference in the static lexical levels of the variable reference and the variable declaration, and associates it with the reference. This difference represents the number of steps to be made along the static chain to reach the activation record of the block which contains the variable declaration. In this way, we avoid searching the activation records in the static link chain.

Various lexical level addressing mechanisms have been proposed [De Prycker, 1982a], [Tanenbaum, 1978]. The evaluation of the performance of the different implementations is based upon statistics on the variable accesses and the block activations and deactivations. These statistics include the distribution of the local, global and intermediate accesses and the average lexical level distance between the point of use and the point of declaration of the program entities.

9.2 GENERATING EXECUTION PROFILES

In Section 9.1 we stressed the importance of execution profiling in the detection of performance bugs. In this section, we show the PDE command language applied to the generation of profiles, at the level of the subprogram calls and at the level of the number of statements executed in a given subprogram.

Problem 9.1

In the program *ResMgmt* introduced in Chapter 2 (see Figure 2.1), we want to count the calls to the subprograms *Init*, *Get* and *Release*.

Solution:

[:*ResMgmt*$1 ->] **allocate** CINIT, CGET, \   (1)
   CRELEASE : INTEGER
[*Init*$1 ->] CINIT := CINIT + 1   (2)
[*Get*$1 ->] CGET := CGET + 1   (3)
[*Release*$1 ->] CRELEASE := CRELEASE + 1   (4)
[:*ResMgmt*$1!T ->] **rput** CINIT, CGET, CRELEASE   (5)

The integer registers CINIT, CGET and CRELEASE are counters of the calls to the subprograms *Init*, *Get* and *Release*, respectively. When the program execution begins, directive (1) allocates these registers and initializes them to zero. When *Init* is executed, directive (2) increases CINIT by one. Similar actions are carried out by directives (3) and (4) for *Get* and *Release*, respectively. When the program execution ends, directive (5) produces the desired display.

Problem 9.2

In the program *Factorials* introduced in Chapter 2 (see Figure 2.9), we want to count the total number of statements executed in the first activation and in each subsequent recursive activation of the recursive function *Fact*, for each call to the function.

Solution:

[*Fact*~1$1 ->] **allocate** COUNT : INTEGER   (1)
[*Fact*$1** ->] COUNT := COUNT + 1   (2)
[*Fact*~1$1!T ->] **rput** COUNT   (3)

When the execution of the first activation of *Fact* begins, directive (1) allocates the integer register COUNT and initializes it to zero. As soon as each statement of *Fact* is executed, directive (2) increases COUNT by one. When the execution of *Fact* ends, directive (3) displays the desired result.

9.3   EVALUATING MEMORY USAGE

The number of accesses made to sensitive data structures is a significant parameter in characterizing program usage of memory resources [Ferrari, 1978]. In this section, we consider the problem of evaluating parameters of this type for the accesses to the shared memory areas.

Problem 9.3

In the program *Sharing* introduced in Chapter 7 (see Figure 7.1), we want to evaluate the number of accesses to the program variable *shared*, which are read and write accesses, made by the process *Increaser*. We want to display the result of this evaluation periodically, the period being expressed in terms of the total number of these accesses.

Solution:

```
        allocate INCR : BOOLEAN
        allocate TOTAL, RACC, WACC : INTEGER
        [ Increaser$1 -> ] rget TOTAL                    (1)
        [ Increaser$4!T -> ] INCR := TRUE                (2)
INCR    [ :Sharing:shared!R -> ] RACC := RACC + 1        (3)
INCR    [ :Sharing:shared!W -> ] WACC := WACC + 1        (4)
        [ Increaser$6!T -> ] INCR := FALSE               (5)
RACC + WACC = TOTAL [ -> ] {                             (6)
        rput RACC/TOTAL, WACC/TOTAL
        RACC := 0; WACC := 0
        }
```

The integer register TOTAL contains the display period. The integer registers RACC and WACC are counters of the read and the write accesses which are performed by *Increaser* to *shared*. As soon as the execution of *Increaser* begins, directive (1) reads the display period from the console and stores it in TOTAL. Directives (3) and (4) increase RACC and WACC on each read and write access to *shared*, respectively. The Boolean register INCR is used (in the guard of these directives) to limit access counting to the accesses performed by *Increaser*. Directives (2) and (5) set and clear INCR when *Increaser* completes the execution of a *P* and a *V* operation on the semaphore *mutex*, respectively. When the total number of accesses to *shared*, as expressed by the sum of the contents of RACC and WACC, equals the display period, directive (6) displays the desired results, expressed by the ratios RACC/TOTAL and WACC/TOTAL, and then clears RACC and WACC.

This solution can be extended to evaluate the number of accesses to *shared* which are due to the activities of the processes *Decreaser* and *Consumer*. This extension can easily be imagined and is not shown.

9.4 CHARACTERIZING PROGRAM STRUCTURE

As seen in Section 9.1, the distribution of the local, global and intermediate accesses, and the average lexical level distance between the point of use and the point of declaration of the program entities may heavily influence the performance of the memory addressing mechanisms. These parameters are strictly connected to the syntactic structure of the program [De Prycker, 1982b]. Problems 9.4 to 9.6 evaluate these statistics of the program structure.

Problem 9.4

When executing the program *ResMgmt*, we want to evaluate the distribution of the local, the global and the intermediate variable accesses.

Solution:

```
[ :ResMgmt$1 -> ] allocate CURRENT, ACC, \          (1)
  LACC, GACC : INTEGER
[ :ResMgmt:BLKR$1** -> ] CURRENT := _SLL            (2)
[ :ResMgmt:BLKR:VAR!RW -> ] {                       (3)
  ACC := ACC + 1
  switch
    case _SLL = 0 :
      GACC := GACC + 1
    case _SLL = CURRENT :
      LACC := LACC + 1
```

end switch
  }
  [:*ResMgmt*$1!T ->] **rput** LACC/ACC, \   (4)
    GACC/ACC, (ACC - LACC - GACC)/ACC

As a consequence of the Pascal scope rules, if a statement generates an access to a given variable, and the static lexical level of this variable is the same as that of the block of the statement, then the variable is local to this block (any variable declared in a different block at the same static lexical level is not visible). This solution takes advantage of this fact and uses the static lexical level register _SLL. As seen in Section 4.4, at any given program cycle this special register contains the static lexical level of the block which contains the declaration of the program entity involved in that cycle.

The integer register CURRENT contains the static lexical level of the block which contains the current statement. The integer register ACC is a counter of the variable accesses, and the integer registers LACC and GACC are counters of the local and the global accesses, respectively. As soon as each program statement is executed, directive (2) stores the static lexical level of the block which contains this statement in CURRENT. On each reference to a program variable, directive (3) increases the value of ACC by one. If the static lexical level of the block which contains the declaration of this variable is zero, this directive increases the value of GACC by one. Whereas, if this static lexical level is the same as the one in the block which contains the current statement, the increase involves the value of LACC. When the program terminates, directive (4) displays the desired results.

Problem 9.5

In the program *ResMgmt*, we want to evaluate the maximum and the average difference between the static lexical levels of the point of access to, and the point of declaration of, the variables involved in the intermediate accesses.

Solution:

  [:*ResMgmt*$1 ->] **allocate** CURRENT, IACC, \   (1)
    MAXDIFF, DIFF, LDIFF : INTEGER

[:*ResMgmt*:BLKR$1** ->] CURRENT := _SLL   (2)
[:*ResMgmt*:BLKR:VAR!RW ->] \   (3)
  switch
    case (_SLL > 0) **and** (_SLL < CURRENT) :
     IACC := IACC + 1
     LDIFF := CURRENT - _SLL
     DIFF := DIFF + LDIFF
     switch
      case MAXDIFF < LDIFF :
       MAXDIFF := LDIFF
     end switch
    end switch
[:*ResMgmt*$1!T ->] **rput** MAXDIFF, DIFF/IACC   (4)

The integer register CURRENT stores the static lexical level of the block which contains the current statement. The integer register IACC is a counter of the intermediate accesses generated by the execution of the program, and the integer register MAXDIFF contains the maximum difference between the static lexical levels of the point of access and the point of declaration of the variables accessed.

Directive (2) updates CURRENT as soon as each program statement is executed. At each variable access, if the involved variable is neither global nor local, directive (3) increases the value of IACC by one, and the value of the integer register DIFF by the difference LDIFF between the static lexical levels of the point of access, as specified by CURRENT, and the point of declaration of the variable, as specified by _SLL. Then, the value stored in MAXDIFF is compared with, and if necessary replaced by, the difference LDIFF. As soon as the program execution ends, directive (4) displays the desired results expressed by the value stored in MAXDIFF and by the ratio DIFF/IACC.

Problem 9.6

In executing the program *ResMgmt*, the directives which follow evaluate the average static lexical level of the subprograms called:

[:*ResMgmt*$1 ->] **allocate** CALLS, \   (1)
  LEVELS : INTEGER

```
[ :ResMgmt:BLKR$1 -> ] {                              (2)
   CALLS := CALLS + 1
   LEVELS := LEVELS + _SLL
   }
[ :ResMgmt$1!T -> ] rput LEVELS/(CALLS - 1)          (3)
```

The integer registers CALLS and LEVELS respectively store the total number of subprogram calls and the sum of the static lexical levels of the subprograms called. As soon as the first statement of a subprogram is executed, directive (2) increases CALLS by one, and LEVELS by the static lexical level of the subprogram block, as specified by the contents of the static lexical level register _SLL. When the program execution ends, directive (3) displays the desired result on the console.

9.5 EVALUATING THE DYNAMIC SUBPROGRAM NESTING DEPTH

As seen in Section 9.1, the memory space requirements of a program are a function of the maximum number of subprogram activations in existence at the same time. Problem 9.7 is concerned with the measurement of this factor for a recursive subprogram.

Problem 9.7

In the program *Factorials*, we want to evaluate the maximum number of activations of the function *Fact* generated in the same recursive execution of the function.

Solution:

```
[ :Factorials$1 -> ] allocate ACT, \                  (1)
   MAXACT : INTEGER
[ Fact$1 -> ] ACT := ACT + 1                          (2)
[ Fact~1$1!T -> ] {                                   (3)
   switch
     case ACT > MAXACT :
       MAXACT := ACT
```

      end switch
      ACT := 0
      }
    [:*Factorials*$1!T ->] **rput** MAXACT   (4)

The integer register ACT is a counter of the number of activations of *Fact*, and the integer register MAXACT contains the result of this experiment. When a new activation of *Fact* is generated, directive (2) increases the value of ACT by one. When the recursive execution of *Fact* is completed, if the new value of ACT is greater than that stored in MAXACT, directive (3) updates MAXACT. Then, this directive clears ACT. When the execution of *Factorials* ends, directive (4) displays the value of MAXACT.

9.6 COMMUNICATION STATISTICS

In a concurrent program, several processes produce resource demands. The fact that further time and space costs originate from the activities connected with interprocess synchronization and communication makes evaluating the performance of this type of program more difficult. We will evaluate a number of statistics on the activities of message delivery and receipt in message-passing programs.

Problem 9.8

In the program *Buffering*, introduced in Chapter 8 (see Figure 8.1), we want to evaluate which fraction of the messages received by the process *BB* have been sent by *Producer1*. We want to display the results of this evaluation periodically, the period being expressed in terms of the total number of messages received by *BB*.

Solution:

      allocate PERIOD, TOTAL, COUNT : INTEGER
      [*BB*$1 ->] **rget** PERIOD   (1)
      [*BB*$6!T, *BB*$9!T ->] TOTAL := TOTAL + 1   (2)
      [*BB*$6!T ->] COUNT := COUNT + 1   (3)
    TOTAL = PERIOD [->] {   (4)

```
rput COUNT/TOTAL
TOTAL := 0; COUNT := 0
}
```

As soon as the execution of *BB* begins, directive (1) reads the display period from the console and stores it in the register PERIOD. The registers TOTAL and COUNT are used to count the messages received by *BB*, and those received by *BB* from *Producer1*, respectively. These two registers are updated by directives (2) and (3). When the total number of messages received by *BB* equals the display period, directive (4) produces the desired display and then clears TOTAL and COUNT.

Problem 9.9

In the program *Buffering* we want to evaluate how many times each branch of the non-deterministic statement *BB$5* is chosen. We want to display the results of this evaluation periodically, in terms of fractions of the total number of iterations of the statement *BB$5*.

Solution:

```
        allocate PERIOD, C1, C2, C3 : INTEGER
        [ BB$1 -> ] rget PERIOD                              (1)
        [ BB$6!T -> ] C1 := C1 + 1                           (2)
        [ BB$9!T -> ] C2 := C2 + 1                           (3)
        [ BB$12!T -> ] C3 := C3 + 1                          (4)
   C1 + C2 + C3 = PERIOD [ -> ] {                            (5)
        rput C1/PERIOD, C2/PERIOD, C3/PERIOD
        C1 := 0; C2 := 0; C3 := 0
        }
```

As soon as the execution of *BB* begins, directive (1) reads the display period from the console and stores it in the register PERIOD. The registers C1, C2 and C3 count the number of times the first, second and third branch of the iterative statement *BB$5* is selected. These counters are updated by directives (2) to (4) when the execution of the message passing statement in the statement guard of the corresponding branch ends. Directive (5) produces the desired display and then clears C1, C2 and C3 when the total number of non-deterministic selections, as expressed by the sum of the values of the three counters, equals the display period.

Problem 9.10

In the program *Wakeup* introduced in Chapter 8 (see Figure 8.2), we evaluate: *(a)* the maximum number of wake-up requests contained in the queue *wakeupq* at the same time; and *(b)* the maximum and the average number of messages which are generated to wake up the clients on every new occasion. We want to display these results periodically, the period being expressed in terms of the total number of wake-up requests inserted into *wakeupq* for case *(a)*, and of the total number of occasions for case *(b)*.

Solution: *(a)*

```
allocate PERIOD, TOTAL, REQ, \
   MAXREQ : INTEGER
[ AC$1 -> ] rget PERIOD                          (1)
[ Insert$1!T -> ] {                              (2)
   REQ := REQ + 1
   TOTAL := TOTAL + 1
   switch
     case REQ > MAXREQ :
       MAXREQ := REQ
   end switch
   }
[ Extract$1!T -> ] REQ := REQ - 1                (3)
TOTAL = PERIOD [ -> ] {                          (4)
     rput MAXREQ
     TOTAL := 0; REQ := 0; MAXREQ := 0
     }
```

PERIOD contains the display period, TOTAL is a counter of the insertions into *wakeupq*, REQ is a counter of the wake-up requests contained in *wakeupq* at the same time and, finally, MAXREQ contains the maximum value assumed by REQ.

When the execution of the process *AC* begins, directive (1) reads the display period from the console and stores it in PERIOD. Directives (2) and (3) increase and decrease the contents of REQ by one each time *AC* inserts a new wake-up request in, or extracts a wake-up request from, *wakeupq*. For each insertion, directive (2) increases the value of TOTAL by one and, if the new value of REQ is greater than that of MAXREQ, it updates MAXREQ. When the total number of insertions equals the display period, directive (4) displays the value of MAXREQ, and then clears TOTAL, REQ and MAXREQ.

(b)

```
allocate PERIOD, EXTR, MAXEXTR, \
    TEXTR, TOCC : INTEGER
[ AC$1 -> ] rget PERIOD                          (1)
[ AC$6 -> ] EXTR := 0                            (2)
[ AC$7!T -> ] {                                  (3)
    EXTR := EXTR + 1
    TEXTR := TEXTR + 1
    }
[ AC$6!T -> ] {                                  (4)
    switch
      case EXTR > MAXEXTR :
        MAXEXTR := EXTR
    end switch
    TOCC := TOCC + 1
    }
TOCC = PERIOD [ -> ] {                           (5)
    rput MAXEXTR, TEXTR/TOCC
    MAXEXTR := 0; TEXTR := 0; TOCC := 0
    }
```

PERIOD stores the display period, EXTR counts the items extracted from *wakeupq* for each occurrence, and MAXEXTR contains the maximum value assumed by EXTR. Finally, TEXTR and TOCC are counters of the total number of extractions from *wakeupq* and of the total number of occasions.

When the execution of the process *AC* begins, directive (1) reads the display period and stores it in PERIOD. As soon as the execution of the statement *AC*$6 begins, directive (2) clears EXTR. Each time *AC* sends a wake-up signal to a client, directive (3) increases EXTR and TEXTR. When the execution of the statement *AC*$6 ends, if the value of EXTR is greater than that of MAXEXTR, directive (4) updates MAXEXTR, and then increases TOCC by one. When the value of TOCC is equal to the display period, directive (5) displays the results expressed by the contents of MAXEXTR and by the ratio TEXTR/TOCC. Finally, this directive clears MAXEXTR, TEXTR and TOCC.

Syntax of the PDE commands

This appendix gives the syntax of the PDE command language constructs that have been introduced in Part I. The syntactic rules are presented in the order resulting from the corresponding chapter sections. They are expressed in a simple extension of the Backus-Naur form. In this extension, syntactic entities (non-terminal symbols) are denoted by strings enclosed in the angular brackets '<' and '>'. Terminal symbols are denoted by words written in bold face or strings enclosed in quotation marks.

A syntactic rule consists of a non-terminal followed by the symbol '::=' and an equivalent construction expressed in terms of terminals and/or non-terminals. A period terminates the rule. The vertical bar 'I' separates alternative options within a rule, the square brackets '[' and ']' denote optionally and the curly brackets '{' and '}' denote 0 or more repetitions.

The syntactic entities whose name is written in italics are part of the target programming language. Their definition belongs to the syntax of this language, not of PDE.

2.2.1

\<block path name\> ::= \<absolute block path name\>
  | \<relative block path name\>.

\<absolute block path name\> ::= ':' \<block list\>
  [\<activation specifier\>].

\<block list\> ::= \<block\> { ':' \<block\>}.

\<block\> ::= *block identifier* | \<automatic block identifier\>.

2.2.2

\<automatic block identifier\> ::= '#' \<unsigned integer\>.

2.2.3

\<multiple block specifier\> ::= 'BLK' | 'BLKR'.

2.2.4

\<activation specifier\> ::= '~' \<unsigned integer\> | '~~'.

2.3, 2.3.1

\<variable name\> ::= \<block path name\>
  [':' \<multiple block specifier\>] ':' \<variable\>.

\<variable\> ::= *variable identifier*
  | *formal subprogram parameter identifier*
  | *function identifier* | \<multiple variable specifier\>.

2.3.2

\<multiple variable specifier\> ::= 'VAR'.

2.4

\<constant name\> ::= \<block path name\>
  [':' \<multiple block specifier\>] ':' \<constant\>.

\<constant\> ::= *constant identifier* | \<multiple constant specifier\>.

\<multiple constant specifier\> ::= 'CONST'.

2.5

\<type name\> ::= \<block path name\>
  [':' \<multiple block specifier\>] ':' \<type\>.

\<type\> ::= *\<type identifier\>* | \<multiple type specifier\>.

\<multiple type specifier\> ::= 'TYPE'.

2.6

\<statement name\> ::= \<labelled statement name\>
  | \<unlabelled statement name\>.

\<labelled statement name\> ::= \<block path name\> '@'
  \<statement label\> [\<multiple statement specifier\>].

\<unlabelled statement name\> ::= \<block path name\> ['@']
  \<automatic statement label\> [\<multiple statement specifier\>].

\<automatic statement label\> ::= '$' \<unsigned integer\> | '$$'.

2.6.1

\<multiple statement specifier\> ::= '*' | '**'.

2.7.1

\<set command\> ::= **set** \<variable name\> **to**
  \<program expression\>.

2.7.2

\<get command\> ::= **get** \<variable name\> { ',' \<variable name\>}
  [**from** \<file\>].

\<file\> ::= \<file identifier\> | 'CONSOLE'.

\<put command\> ::= **put** *\<program expression\>*
  { ',' *\<program expression\>*} [**append**] [**to** \<file\>].

2.7.3

\<permanent input command\> ::= **permanent input** \<file\>.

\<permanent output command\> ::= **permanent output** \<file\>.

2.8

<alias command> ::= **alias** <alias identifier> ':='
  <block path name>.

<alias display command> ::= **alias display** [**append**] [**to** <file>].

<unalias command> ::= **unalias** <alias identifier>
  { ',' <alias identifier>}.

<unalias all command> ::= **unalias all**.

3.1

<access> ::= <elementary access> | <multiple access>.

<elementary access> ::= <variable access> | <constant access>
  | <type access> | <statement access>.

<multiple access> ::= <elementary access>
  { ',' <elementary access>}.

3.1.1

<variable access> ::= <variable name>
  ['!' <variable access mode>].

<variable access mode> ::= 'R' | 'W' | 'RW'.

3.1.2

<constant access> ::= <constant name>
  ['!' <constant access mode>].

<constant access mode> ::= 'R'.

3.1.3

<type access> ::= <type name> ['!' <type access mode>].

<type access mode> ::= 'R' | 'W' | 'RW'.

3.1.4

<statement access> ::= <statement name>
  ['!' <statement access mode>].

<statement access mode> ::= 'B' | 'T'.

3.2

<conditional> ::= *<Boolean program expression>*.

<event> ::= '['[<access>] '->' [<conditional>]']'.

4.1

<register> ::= <general register > | <special register>.

<general register> ::= <user-defined register>
  | <predefined register>.

<special register> ::= <block pointer> | <statement pointer>
  | <additional special register>.

<additional special register> ::= (implementation dependent).

4.1.1

<allocate command> ::= **allocate** <user-defined register list> ':'
  <scalar type> ['(' <integer expression> ')'].

<user-defined register list> ::= <user-defined register>
  {',' <user-defined register>}.

<scalar type> ::= 'INTEGER' | 'REAL' | 'BOOLEAN'
  | 'CHARACTER'.

<delete command> ::= **delete** <user-defined register list>.

4.1.2

<predefined register> ::= <upper case letter> '%' ['R' | 'B' | 'C'].

4.2.1, 4.2.2

<block pointer> ::= [<process name>] '^'.

<process name> ::= <statement name> '|' | <block path name> '|'.

4.2.3

<relative block path name> ::= [<block pointer>
  [<pointer modifier>]] <block list> [<activation specifier>].

<pointer modifier> ::= '^' {'^'}.

4.3.1, 4.3.2

<statement pointer> ::= [<process name>] <block path name> '@'.

4.3.4

<current statement pointer> ::= [<process name>] '@'.

4.5.1

<assignment command> ::= <register> ':=' <scalar expression>.

4.5.2

<rget command> ::= **rget** <register> {',' <register>}
[**from** <file>].

<rput command> ::= **rput** <rput parameter> {',' <rput parameter>}
[**append**] [**to** <file>].

<rput parameter> ::= <scalar expression> | <special register>
| <string literal>.

4.5.4

<rset command> ::= **rset** <variable name> **to** <scalar expression>.

5.1

<command> ::= <simple command> | <structured command>.

<simple command> ::= <activate command> | <alias command>
| <alias display command> | <allocate command>
| <assignment command> | <break command>
| <default group command> | <delete command>
| <directive display command> | <exec command>
| <exit command> | <get command>
| <group command> | <group display command>
| <permanent input command> | <permanent output command>
| <put command> | <rget command>
| <rput command> | <rset command>
| <run command> | <set command>
| <terminate command> | <unalias command>
| <unalias all command> | <ungroup command>.

<structured command> ::= <compound command>
| <selection command> | <repetition command>.

5.1.1

<compound command> ::= '{' <command sequence> '}'.

<command sequence> ::= <command> {<command separator>
<command>}.

<command separator> ::= ';' | <new line>.

5.1.2

<selection command> ::= **switch** <switch element>
{<switch element>} **end switch**.

<switch element> ::= **case** <condition> ':' <command sequence>.

<condition> ::= <Boolean expression>.

5.1.3

<repetition command> ::= **loop** <command sequence> **end loop**.

<exit command> ::= **exit** [<condition>].

5.1.4

<command script> ::= **script** <command script identifier>
'{' <command sequence> '}'.

<exec command> ::= **exec** <command script identifier>.

5.2

<directive> ::= <simple directive> | <guarded directive>.

<simple directive> ::= <event> <command>.

<guarded directive> ::= <guard> <event> <command>.

<guard> ::= <Boolean expression>.

5.2.1

<activate command> ::= [**activate**] <directive>.

<terminate command> ::= **terminate** <directive number list>.

\<directive number list\> ::= \<directive number specification\>
{ ',' \<directive number specification\> }.

\<directive number specification\> ::= \<directive number\>
| \<directive number range\>.

\<directive number\> ::= \<unsigned integer\> | '~'.

\<directive number range\> ::= \<directive number\> '..'
\<directive number\>.

5.2.3

\<directive display command\> ::= **directive display**
\<directive number list\> [**append**] [**to** \<file\>].

5.3.1, 5.3.2

\<break command\> ::= **break** [\<process list\>].

\<process list\> ::= \<process list element\>
{ ',' \<process list element\> } | 'ALL'.

\<process list element\> ::= \<process name\> | \<group identifier\>.

\<run command\> ::= **run** [\<process list\>].

5.3.3

\<group command\> ::= **group** \<group identifier\> ':='
\<process list\>.

\<default group command\> ::= **default group** \<group identifier\>.

\<ungroup command\> ::= **ungroup** \<group identifier\>
{ ',' \<group identifier\> }.

\<group display command\> ::= **group display** [**append**]
[**to** \<file\>].

Glossary

Absolute block path name: The name of a block expressed in reference to the program tree representation, by the list of the identifiers of the blocks in the path from the root of the tree to this block.

Absolute block path name notation: A notation which identifies the blocks of the target program by absolute block path names.

Access: The specification of an operation occurring as a consequence of the execution of the target program.

Access mode: The specification of a subset of the set of the operations which can be performed on a program entity of a given class.

Access-mode check: A check to detect any violation of given access mode constraints concerning a target entity.

Accumulated trap: A trap which is triggered by the nth occurrence of a given event.

Activation record: A data structure containing all the information needed to execute a program block. It is created when a new block instance is generated.

Activation specifier: An extension of the block path name notation to denote recursive block activations.

Active directive: A directive which is processed concurrently with the execution of the target program, according to the values assumed by the program entities and by the registers included in the directive specification.

Aggregate constructor: A programming language construct used to define composite types in terms of other scalar or composite types. Examples are the array and record constructors.

Alias: An identifier used as a substitute of a block path name.

Array register: A register consisting of a fixed number of elements of the same scalar type.

Assertion: A logical predicate defined in terms of the state of the program and/or of PDE.

Asynchronous break trap: A break trap caused by the programmer from the console.

Asynchronous communication: A form of interprocess communication in which the execution of a *send* operation does not delay the sender. The execution of the sender can always proceed immediately after the message has been delivered.

Automatic block identifier: An identifier which is associated by PDE with each nameless block.

Automatic trace: A trace recorded in terms of a fixed list of aspects of the target program activity.

Block pointer: A special register containing the path name of the current block. In a concurrent program, PDE associates a block pointer with each process.

Block statement: A programming language notation to indicate nameless blocks.

Block-structured language: A high-level language in which program statements are grouped into blocks by block delimiters.

Bottom-up programming methodology: A program development methodology in which a large program is partitioned into program layers, organized hierarchically.

Breakpoint: A synchronous break trap caused by the execution of a given program statement.

Break state: The state of a process whose elaborations have been suspended by a break trap.

Break trap: A permanent deviation in the normal control flow of the target program which suspends the program execution. In a concurrent program, a break trap suspends one or more processes generated by the execution of the program.

Buffered communication: A form of interprocess communication in which a buffer with a bounded capacity is associated with the communication link.

Client/server relationship: An interprocess relationship in which a server process provides service to a number of client processes.

Command: The specification of an action to be performed by PDE, expressed in terms of manipulation of one or more registers and/or program entities.

Command script: A PDE construct to associate an identifier with a sequence of commands.

Communication link: A logical connection between two processes.

Competition: A form of interprocess interaction in which each process has exclusive access to shared resources.

Concurrent program: A set of sequential processes whose executions can overlap in time.

Conditional: A Boolean expression whose value depends on the state of the target program.

Control flow: The sequence of the statements of the target program which are executed as a consequence of the program activity.

Controlled-execution technique: A debugging technique in which the user monitors the behaviour of the target program interactively, by means of break traps.

Control path monitoring: A debugging technique which ascertains whether given control paths of a program have been executed or not.

Cooperation: A form of interprocess interaction in which the processes exchange information to achieve a common goal.

Critical section: A sequence of statements which must be executed as an indivisible operation.

Current block: The target program block containing the current statement. In a concurrent program, the current block of a given process is the block containing the current statement of this process.

Current statement: The statement currently being executed in a given program cycle. In a concurrent program, the current statement of a given process is the statement being executed by this process.

Current statement pointer: A notation to identify the current statement.

Cyclical debugging: A debugging method consisting of repeating the execution of a program with appropriate test data until the bug has been eliminated.

Data type: The specification of a set of values and the set of possible operations on these values.

Deadlock: A circular wait condition in which every member of a process set has obtained exclusive access to a shared resource, and needs an additional resource which is allocated to the next member of the set.

Debugging: The process of diagnosing, locating and removing program errors.

Debugging experiment: A set of tests aimed at obtaining answers to questions concerning the program behaviour.

Debugging probe: One or more statements added at an appropriate point in the source code of the target program and aimed at capturing debugging information.

Direct asymmetric communication: A form of interprocess communication in which only the sender specifies the intended receiver; whereas the receiver obtains the name of the sender as an output parameter of the *receive* operation.

Direct symmetric communication: A form of interprocess communication in which each process explicitly names the other as the destination or the source in a *send* or a *receive* operation.

Directive: The specification of a command to be conditionally executed on the occurrence of a given event.

Directive number: A number associated with a directive on its activation in order to identify the directive.

Directive script: A command script including one or more **activate** commands.

Dynamic statement ordering: The ordering of the target program statements resulting from dynamic program activity.

Elementary access: An access specified in terms of the name of a program entity and an access mode.

Enumeration type: A data type defined by declaring the identifiers of the values of the type and an ordering relation among these values.

Equivalent accesses: Two accesses which are produced at the same program cycles.

Event: The specification of an access and a conditional.

Execution monitor: A debugging tool aimed at supporting trace gathering.

Execution profile: The number of times the different program statements have been executed in a given program run.

Execution profiler: A debugging tool aimed at gathering execution profiles.

Existent variable: A variable for which memory space has been allocated to store its value.

Flow history: The evolution of an aspect of the program state expressed in terms of the path followed by the program control flow.

Flow trace: A trace containing information concerning the program flow history.

General register: A register which is used to store partial results of the PDE experiment.

Global access: An access to a variable declared in the outermost program block.

Guard: A Boolean expression which is part of a guarded directive.

Guarded directive: A directive consisting of the specification of a guard, an event and a command.

Guarded statement: A structured statement consisting of a statement guard and a statement sequence.

Indirect communication: A form of interprocess communication in which processes communicate via mailboxes.

Intermediate access: A variable access which is neither a local access nor a global access.

Local access: An access to a variable performed by a statement declared in the same block as the variable.

Mailbox: A recipient into which messages can be inserted and from which messages can be extracted.

Message passing: A form of interprocess communication based on the sending and receipt of messages.

Monitor: A programming language construct which implements the abstract type of a shared resource.

Monitoring phase: When a concurrent program is being debugged, the phase of a cyclical debugging experiment in which we collect the replay trace.

Multiple access: An access specified in terms of two or more elementary accesses.

Multiple block notation: A notation for identifying all the blocks declared in a given block, and all the blocks declared in these blocks, recursively.

Multiple constant notation: A notation for identifying all the constants defined in a given block.

Multiple statement notation: A notation for identifying all the statements which compound a given statement, and all the statements which compound these statements, recursively.

Multiple type notation: A notation for identifying all the types defined in a given block.

Multiple variable notation: A notation for identifying all the variables defined in a given block.

Naming rules: The rules used by PDE to denote the program entities.

Open directive: An active directive which is either a simple directive or a guarded directive whose guard is true.

Performance bug: The cause of a limitation in the performance of the target program.

Pipeline: A sequence of two or more concurrent processes such that each process receives its input from the preceding one and sends its output to the following one.

Pointer modifier: A notation for moving the starting block of the tree path specified by a relative path name to an ancestor of the current block.

Port: A mailbox which holds messages of a specific type.

Predefined register: A general register which is allocated and initialized by PDE at the beginning of the PDE session.

Process declaration: A notation for specifying concurrent execution at the block level.

Profiling: A program performance evaluation technique which uses execution profiles to identify the performance bugs.

Program cycle: Any aspect of the execution of the target program which causes an operation to be performed on a program entity.

Program state: The values of the program-defined entities and the point reached by the program control flow.

Receive operation: An operation which can be used by a process to receive a message from another process, a mailbox or a port.

Register: A visible portion of the private storage of PDE.

Relative block path name: The name of a block expressed in reference to the program tree representation, by the list of the identifiers of the blocks in the path from the current block to this block.

Relative block path name notation: A notation which identifies the blocks of the target program by relative block path names.

Remote procedure: A procedure which is executed in a different process, possibly on a separate computer.

Replay phase: When a concurrent program is being debugged, the phase of a cyclical debugging experiment in which the program is rerun with the same input data, and the contents of the replay trace are used to drive the non-sequential aspects of the program execution.

Replay trace: In a cyclical debugging experiment involving a concurrent program, a trace which contains the sequence of the process interactions and the data values associated with these interactions.

Reproducible behaviour: The behaviour of a program which produces the same state and flow histories when repeatedly executed with the same given set of input data.

Run state: The state of a process which is carrying on the elaborations specified by the source program.

Scalar register: A register which is a recipient for a single value of a scalar type.

Scope rules: The rules of the programming language which identify the subset of the program entities that are visible in any given block.

Selective trace: A trace recorded in terms of only those aspects of the target program activity which are of specific interest to the tracing experiment being performed.

Semaphore: A mechanism for programming mutual exclusion and interprocess synchronization.

Send operation: An operation which can be used by a process to send a message to another process, a mailbox or a port.

Shared variable: A variable which is accessible by two or more processes which compound a concurrent program.

Simple command: A command expressing an elementary PDE action.

Simple directive: A directive consisting of the specification of an event and a command.

Single-step execution: The ability to generate a break trap on the execution of every program statement or of every statement of a given program fragment.

Special register: A register containing information on an aspect of the state of the target program. Its value is updated automatically by PDE during program execution, according to the evolution of the program activity.

State-based debugging: A debugging approach in which the dynamics of the target program is observed from the point of view of the program state.

State history: The evolution of an aspect of the program state expressed in terms of the values assumed by a subset of the program-defined entities.

Statement guard: A part of a guarded statement consisting of a Boolean expression and a synchronous message-passing operation.

Statement pointer: A special register which is associated with each block of the target program, and contains the name of the statement executed most recently in this block. In a concurrent program, if a block is shared between two or more processes, a statement pointer is associated with this block for each of these processes.

State trace: A trace containing information concerning the program state history.

Static lexical level: In the tree representation of a program, the distance, i.e. the number of program blocks, between a given block and the root of the tree.

Static lexical level register: A special register which, in any given program cycle, records the static lexical level of the block containing the declaration of the program entity involved in the program operation performed at that cycle.

Static program structure: The structure of the target program as specified by the source program text.

Stepwise execution: A debugging technique in which traps are generated periodically.

Structured command: A command expressing a composite PDE action in terms of other simple or structured commands.

Subrange type: A scalar type whose values are a subset of the set of the values of another scalar type.

Synchronous break trap: A break trap caused by an aspect of the target program activity.

Synchronous communication: A form of interprocess communication in which the first of the two communicating processes which executes a message-passing operation must wait for the other process to arrive at the communication point.

Target program: The program being developed in the current PDE session.

Textual order number: The order number of a given entity of the target program in the source program text.

Timing error: A situation in which process interactions take place in an unexpected order.

Trace: The result of the information gathering actions generated by a sequence of trace traps.

Trace trap: A temporary deviation in the normal control flow of the target program which causes the information concerning an aspect of the program state to be collected.

Tracing technique: A debugging technique based on traces.

Trap: A permanent or temporary deviation in the normal control flow of the target program.

Tree representation: A representation of the static nesting of the blocks of a program written in a block-structured language.

Undefined block path name: The initial value of a block pointer.

Undefined statement name: The initial value of a statement pointer.

User-defined register: A general register which is allocated and deleted by the programmer.

Value-range check: A check aimed at detecting any violation of given in-range or out-of-range constraints concerning the value of a target entity.

Visible entity: A program entity which can be named in the current block, according to the scope rules of the target program.

Bibliography

Aho, A. V., R. Sethi and J. D. Ullman, *Compilers, Principles, Techniques, and Tools*. Reading: Addison-Wesley, 1986.

Andrews, G. R. and F. B. Schneider, "Concepts and notations for concurrent programming," *ACM Computing Surveys*, vol. 15, no. 1, pp. 3–43, March 1983.

ANSI, "Reference manual for the Ada programming language," ANSI/MIL-STD 1815 A, American National Standards Institute, Washington, D.C., January 1983.

Ben-Ari, M., *Principles of Concurrent and Distributed Programming*. New York: Prentice Hall, 1990.

Bhatt, D. and M. Schroeder, "A comprehensive approach to instrumentation for experimentation in a distributed computing environment," in *Proceedings of the Third International Conference on Distributed Computing Systems*, Miami, Florida, pp. 330–340, October 1982.

Binder, R., *Application Debugging*. Englewood Cliffs: Prentice-Hall, 1985.

Brinch Hansen, P., *Operating Systems Principles*. Englewood Cliffs: Prentice-Hall, 1973.

Brinch Hansen, P., "The programming language Concurrent Pascal," *IEEE Transactions on Software Engineering*, vol. SE-1, no. 2, pp. 199–207, June 1975.

Brinch Hansen, P., "Edison – A multiprocessor language," *Software – Practice and Experience*, vol. 11, no. 4, pp. 325–361, April 1981.

Cheung, W. H., J. P. Black and E. Manning, "A framework for distributed debugging," *IEEE Software*, vol. 7, no. 1, pp. 106–115, January 1990.

De Blasi, M., *Computer Architecture*. Wokingham: Addison-Wesley, 1990.

De Prycker, M., "A performance analysis of the implementation of addressing methods in block-structured languages," *IEEE Transactions on Computers*, vol. C-31, no. 2, pp. 155–163, February 1982a.

De Prycker, M., "On the development of a measurement system for high level language program statistics," *IEEE Transactions on Computers*, vol. C-31, no. 9, pp. 883–891, September 1982b.

Dijkstra, E. W., "Guarded commands, nondeterminacy, and formal derivation of programs," *Communications of the ACM*, vol. 18, no. 8, pp. 453–457, August 1975.

Einbu, J., *A Program Architecture for Improved Maintainability in Software Engineering*. Chichester: Ellis Horwood, 1989.

Elliot, B., "A high-level debugger for PL/I, Fortran and Basic," *Software – Practice and Experience*, vol. 12, no. 4, pp. 331–340, April 1982.

Fairley, R., *Software Engineering Concepts*. New York: McGraw-Hill, 1985.

Feldman, M. B., "Data abstraction, structured programming, and the practicing programmer," *Software – Practice and Experience*, vol. 11, no. 7, pp. 697–710, July 1981.

Feldman, M. B., *Data Structures With Modula-2*. London: Prentice-Hall, 1988.

Ferrari, D., *Computer Systems Performance Evaluation*. Prentice-Hall, 1978.

Findlay, W. and D. A. Watt, *Pascal: An Introduction to Methodical Programming.* London: Pitman, 1985.

Foxley, E. and D. J. Morgan, "Monitoring the run-time activity of Algol 68-R programs," *Software – Practice and Experience,* vol. 8, no. 1, pp. 29–34, January–February 1978.

Gait, J., "A debugger for concurrent programs," *Software – Practice and Experience,* vol. 15, no. 6, pp. 539–554, June 1985.

Garcia-Molina, H., F. Germano and W. H. Kohler, "Debugging a distributed computing system," *IEEE Transactions on Software Engineering,* vol. SE-10, no. 2, pp. 210–219, March 1984.

Ghezzi, C. and M. Jazayeri, *Programming Language Concepts,* Second Edition. New York: John Wiley & Sons, 1987.

Gondzio, M., "Microprocessor debugging techniques and their application in debugger design," *Software – Practice and Experience,* vol. 17, no. 3, pp. 215–226, March 1987.

Griffin, J. H., H. J. Wasserman and L. P. McGavran, "A debugger for parallel processes," *Software – Practice and Experience,* vol. 18, no. 12, pp. 1179–1190, December 1988.

Guttag, J., "Abstract data types and the development of data structures," *Communications of the ACM,* vol. 20, no. 6, pp. 396–404, June 1977.

Hoare, C. A. R., "Monitors: An operating system structuring concept," *Communications of the ACM,* vol. 17, no. 10, pp. 549–557, October 1974.

Jensen, K. and N. Wirth, *Pascal User Manual and Report,* Third Edition. New York: Springer Verlag, 1985.

Johnson, M. S., "Some requirements for architectural support of software debugging," in *Proceedings of the Symposium on Architectural Support for Programming Languages and Operating Systems,* Palo Alto, California, March 1982; in *Com-*

puter Architecture News, vol. 10, no. 2, pp. 140–148, March 1982.

Kaner, C., *Testing Computer Software*. Blue Ridge Summit: Tab Books, 1988.

Katevenis, M. G. H., *Reduced Instruction Set Computer Architectures for VLSI*. Cambridge: The MIT Press, 1985.

Koffman, E. B., *Turbo Pascal, A Problem Solving Approach*. Reading: Addison-Wesley, 1986.

Krishnamurthy, E. V., *Parallel Processing: Principles and Practice*. Sydney: Addison-Wesley, 1989.

Lampson, W., J. J. Horning, R. L. London, J. G. Mitchell and G. L. Popek, "Report on the programming language Euclid," *SIGPLAN Notices*, vol. 12, no. 2, February 1977.

Lauesen, S., "Debugging techniques," *Software – Practice and Experience*, vol. 9, no. 1, pp. 51–63, January 1979.

Lazzerini, B., L. Lopriore and C. A. Prete, "A programmable debugging aid for real-time software development," *IEEE Micro*, vol. 6, no. 3, pp. 34–42, June 1986.

Lazzerini, B., "Effective VLSI processor architectures for HLL computers: the RISC approach," *IEEE Micro*, vol. 9, no. 1, pp. 57–65, February 1989a.

Lazzerini, B. and L. Lopriore, "Abstraction mechanisms for event control in program debugging," *IEEE Transactions on Software Engineering*, vol. 15, no. 7, pp. 890–901, July 1989b.

LeBlanc, R. J. and A. D. Robbins, "Event-driven monitoring of distributed programs," in *Proceedings of the Fifth International Conference on Distributed Computing Systems*, Denver, Colorado, pp. 515–522, May 1985.

LeBlanc, T. J. and J. M. Mellor-Crummey, "Debugging parallel programs with instant replay," *IEEE Transactions on Computers*, vol. C-36, no. 4, pp. 471–482, April 1987.

Lopriore, L., "Capability based tagged architectures," *IEEE Transactions on Computers*, vol. C-33, no. 9, pp. 786–803, September 1984.

Lopriore, L., "A user interface specification for a program debugging and measuring environment," *Software – Practice and Experience*, vol. 19, no. 5, pp. 437–460, May 1989.

Maddix, F. and G. Morgan, *Systems Software: An Introduction to Language Processors and Operating Systems*. Chichester: Ellis Horwood, 1989.

McDowell, C. E. and D. P. Helmbold, "Debugging concurrent programs," *ACM Computing Surveys*, vol. 21, no. 4, pp. 593–622, December 1989.

McKerrow, P., *Performance Measurement of Computer Systems*. Sydney: Addison-Wesley, 1988.

Moher, T. G., "PROVIDE: A process visualization and debugging environment," *IEEE Transactions on Software Engineering*, vol. 14, no. 6, pp. 849–857, June 1988.

Moore, L., *Foundations of Programming with Pascal*. Chichester: Ellis Horwood, 1980.

Mullerburg, M. A. F., "The role of debugging within software engineering environments," in *Proceedings of the ACM SIGSOFT/SIGPLAN Software Engineering Symposium on High Level Debugging*, Pacific Grove, California, March 1983; in *Software Engineering Notes*, vol. 8, no. 4, pp. 81–90, August 1983.

Myers, G. J., *Software Reliability: Principles and Practices*. New York: John Wiley & Sons, 1976.

Myers, G. J., *The Art of Software Testing*. New York: John Wiley & Sons, 1979.

Naur, P., Editor, "Revised report on the algorithmic language ALGOL 60," *Communications of the ACM*, vol. 6, no. 1, pp. 1–17, January 1963.

Parrington, N. and M. Roper, *Understanding Software Testing.* Chichester: Ellis Horwood, 1989.

Patterson, D. and C. Sequin, "A VLSI RISC," *Computer*, vol. 15, no. 9, pp. 8–21, September 1982.

Ponder, C. and R. J. Fateman, "Inaccuracies in program profilers," *Software – Practice and Experience*, vol. 18, no. 5, pp. 459–467, May 1988.

Pratt, T. W., *Programming Languages: Design and Implementation.* Englewood Cliffs: Prentice-Hall, 1975.

Seidner, R. and N. Tindall, "Interactive debug requirements," in *Proceedings of the ACM SIGSOFT/SIGPLAN Software Engineering Symposium on High Level Debugging*, Pacific Grove, California, March 1983; in *Software Engineering Notes*, vol. 8, no. 4, pp. 9–22, August 1983.

Shooman, M. L., *Software Engineering.* McGraw-Hill, 1983.

Silberschatz, A., J. L. Peterson and P. Galvin, *Operating System Concepts,* Third Edition. Reading: Addison-Wesley, 1991.

Sommerville, I., *Software Engineering,* Third Edition. Wokingham: Addison-Wesley, 1989.

Tanenbaum, A. S., "Implications of structured programming for machine architecture," *Communications of the ACM*, vol. 21, no. 3, pp. 237–246, March 1978.

Terry, P. D., *Programming Language Translation: A Practical Approach.* Wokingham: Addison-Wesley, 1986.

Terry, P. D., *An Introduction to Programming With Modula-2.* Wokingham: Addison-Wesley, 1987.

Toy, W. and B. Zee, *Computer Hardware/Software Architecture.* Englewood Cliffs: Prentice-Hall, 1986.

van der Linden, F. and I. Wilson, "An interactive debugging environment," *IEEE Micro*, vol. 5, no. 4, pp. 18–31, August 1985.

Watson, D., *High-Level Languages and Their Compilers*. Wokingham: Addison-Wesley, 1989.

Wilson, L. B. and R. G. Clark, *Comparative Programming Languages*. Wokingham: Addison-Wesley, 1988.

Wirth, N., *Programming in Modula-2,* Fourth Edition. Berlin: Springer-Verlag, 1988a.

Wirth, N., "The programming language Oberon," *Software – Practice and Experience*, vol. 18, no. 7, pp. 671–690, July 1988b.

Index

P